table of contents

foreward

*H*i. My name is *Hudson Bundschuh* and I'm a 6th grader. My dad wrote this book and here's what I thought about it. I really liked how my dad knew *exactly* what goes on in middle school. Also I'm really amazed *how* my dad knows so much considering he went to middle school 41 years ago. I also liked the humor my dad put into it. He didn't just put "This is how to make it through middle school. First you get a locker, then you go to your classes, after that its recess." I liked how he made it interesting and funny. It makes me want to read more and more. I also liked the pictures. The pictures (my dad drew them) made the book fun! They are really goofy and well done. So basically what I'm saying is this is a really great book!

*H*ey, this is *Allegra Bundschuh* and I'm in the 8th grade. I'll just tell you that this book is a really big help. Believe me, I know—I didn't survive. Last year I got a D in math for the fourth quarter. If you think that's nothing, you are SO wrong. I got grounded for the WHOLE summer. I am not kidding! I only saw my friends at church. Other than that, no friends. No sleepovers. No nothing. So unless you want to be sitting around your house as I did, take the advice my dad offers in this book. I know I will from now on! (Okay Dad, I wrote something for your book. Can I get off restriction now?)

introduction

*T*his book is especially for you who are starting your exciting and sometimes scary journey through Middle School or Junior High. I'd like to think that this book could be used as a map through a minefield. This book won't keep you from stomping on a nice juicy landmine, if that's what you really want to do—but at least it will show you where most of the landmines are hidden, if you decide to avoid them. Most of the problems that kids like you get themselves into during Middle School can be dodged if you know where to step.

I hope that some of the questions, concerns and doubts that you have about entering this new adventure will be answered as you read through this book. All of the stories are true, even the bizarre ones. I have changed the names of the kids involved, 'cause that's what you're supposed to do when you write a book.

ving middle school

ii

Throughout this book, you will find that I use the term *Middle School* instead of Junior High. For the sake of simplicity, I had to decide what to call the time you spend in school between elementary school and high school—usually somewhere between grades six through nine. For those of you who have never heard of a Middle School—it's just like a Junior High, except it starts with sixth grade rather than seventh, and usually ends with eighth grade instead of ninth.

I wrote this book because I have many young friends who are just starting Middle School and who are concerned about what will happen to them. I'd like to consider you my friend too. If you have questions about Middle School that are not answered in this book, please write to me. I'll be glad to help if I can.

Most of all, I hope this book helps you to see that God can be your best friend and guide through the wild years ahead of you.

Rick Bundschuh
PO Box 633
Lawai, Hawaii 96765
RickBundschuh@mac.com

surviving middle school

chapter one

getting started

I barfed in class. During the first week of first grade, in front of everybody, I spewed. There I was, busily painting fine works of art, when the urge to hurl hit me. I thought I could hold it back, but I was wrong. I puked all over my piece of art (adding far more vivid colors to the painting, but ruining its resale value). My breakfast rolled down the painting, through the paint tray, and into a lumpy puddle on the floor. Everyone stared at the

mess for a few seconds, and then the laughter began—it started with a jug-eared kid in the back of the class and rippled out across the room.

Trudging to the health office, I couldn't believe what had happened. I was crushed, humiliated. The churning in my gut could not compete with the cloud of doom which now hung over me. I knew that my life was ruined.

Since that horrible day, I have managed to pull the mangled remains of my self-esteem back together. But even so, after that experience I faced every new school year and every move to a new school with a sense of dread.

jangled nerves

Feeling nervous when facing a new experience is natural. And Middle School is definitely something new. Lots of kids wonder, "What will happen to me? Will I do or say something that will prove to everyone else that I am some kind of dork or poser?"

Reading this book will not keep you from barfing on your masterpiece—stomachs will do what they must—but it may help you deal with some of the other things that worry you. You will know what to expect, what to do, and in some cases, what to avoid doing.

If you're like me, your very first day of school will probably be scary, so I've written a whole chapter about it. Interested? Let's crack into it!

the BIG day

When your alarm clock buzzes obnoxiously that first morning, you'll already be awake. In fact, I doubt that you'll have gotten much sleep at all, what with thinking about this day: *the first day of school.* Most likely you'll be experiencing some kind of high anxiety. Take a deep breath and try to relax. Chances are that you'll not only survive this new adventure, but you'll enjoy it too—once you get the hang of it.

Reading this book may help you deal with some things that worry you.

The first clue that your life is changing will hit you before you even leave the house—the uncomfortable feel of new stiff clothes (or, for some, uniforms). When you walk on campus, look around and you'll see that just about everyone is experiencing it: pants so stiff they can stand up by themselves, and shoes that are so squeaky clean and sweet smelling that they don't yet attract flies. Colors are brilliant, ketchup stains are absent, and some kids are even walking around with the price tags dangling from their clothing!

Naturally, everyone is trying to make a good first impression. You may feel like laughing at some of their efforts, but you need to realize that this is pretty typical for the first day and you will probably be part of the parade. So, wear your cool new clothes and be careful not to spill stuff on them—at least not today.

lost in a crowd

When you get to school, you'll be surrounded by strangers. That's because a bunch of elementary schools typically feed into one Middle School. Everybody will be spending a lot of time checking everyone else out. Try to keep this process from bothering you—you'll probably be doing a bit of checking yourself! Some kids are overjoyed at the thought of having so many cute boys or girls to choose from. Others worry that they will not be as important in this sea of faces as they were in their comfortable small grade schools.

Relax—really big blunders rarely happen on the first day.

You may be convinced that you will start your first day by doing something that makes you look like a complete moron. Let me reassure you—almost everybody feels self-conscious and out of place, but don't expect him or her to admit it. And relax, really big blunders rarely happen on the first day. You'll have the rest of the school year to make a klutz out of yourself!

scrambled schedules

Now that you're used to being looked over, find out where you're supposed to be and get there. (Well, maybe you had better find the restroom first.) In Middle School you will most likely be assigned a new class, a new room, a new subject and a new teacher for every hour or so of the school day.

Some schools mail your class schedules to you during the summer. Others will simply hang printouts listing student names and the class assignments on hallway bulletin boards. Some schools post notices that direct you to your *Homeroom*, and in your homeroom the teacher hands you your schedule.

If you have a common last name, things can get really confusing at this point. The poor kid whose last name happens to be *Smith* can end up wandering the halls all day, looking for classes that really belong to some other Smith. This can get really upsetting if you find you have been assigned to a boys' gym class—and you're a girl! If something like this happens to you, don't panic and go home. Help is available, and with any luck, your problem should be solved by the end of the semester.

Oh, and one last piece of advice about schedules— write yours down in a notebook just in case you misplace the copy you are handed. If you think you might lose your notebook, write your schedule on your arm. Hopefully, you won't lose that.

finding your way

The *fear of getting lost* rates right up there with the *fear of throwing up in the cafeteria*. But chances are you won't get lost at all. Oh, there may be moments of panic, but little genuine "lost-ness."

MATH CLASS? I THINK YOU MISSED A TURN!

The worst that can happen is that you'll stumble into a class after it has already started. If you enjoy drawing attention to yourself, this won't be a big deal. But if you're trying to develop a cool low-key image, the experience may be very embarrassing. The best you can do is to try to look calm; otherwise everyone will know that you have been desperately wandering the halls.

help wanted

When you needed help in grade school, you could always ask an adult. Adults were easy to spot because they were so much taller than everyone else. But in Middle School, finding an adult by size alone is a bit harder since some kids are already about as tall as their teachers. This means that for you to get an adult's help, you will have to find someone who looks old or has bad hair.

You can always go to the office and ask for help.

If you're really lost, one place that is usually full of adults is the office. You can always go there and ask for help without feeling ashamed or stupid. There's no reason to feel ashamed about going to the office if you can't figure out where you are supposed to be—after all, your friends will be in there asking for help too!

If you'd rather not make trips to the office between all your classes, take heart—you still have other options. One is to follow a friend around. If that friend has figured out the system, you're in luck. If not, at least you'll be lost together. Or you can team up with someone who is one grade above you in school and have that person guide you through the day. Be careful though—some enterprising older kid may charge you for your tour.

first class

Your first class of the morning is usually identified as your "Homeroom." Before you crack open your books, the teacher will take roll, read the announcements and tell you about any upcoming events. Or she may just turn on the TV and do her nails while you watch announcements on the in-house system.

Expect the seating in every class to be about the same. Teachers rarely assign seats, and most of the time finding a seat turns into a free-for-all. You can almost predict where different kids will sit—the dummies will race for the seats farthest back in the class (where they can carve on their desks all year long) and the brains will look for desks right up front. And everyone will sit as far away as possible from the kid who stepped in dog doo on his way to school!

Logic will tell you that if you want the seat of your choice, you should get to class as soon as possible on the first day. But actual experience will probably teach you that you'll just have to take whatever seat is left after you've explored the whole school trying to find your class.

All of your actions in Middle School are directed by bells.

bell ringers

You'll know class has begun when the school bell rings. In fact, you'll probably find that all of your actions in Middle School are directed by bells. They tell when to eat, study, change classes, and go home. If you forget what to do when the bell rings, just follow everyone else and you'll probably be okay.

locker battles

Middle School students can often get relief from their 300-pound backpacks by storing books and gear in a locker. In some schools, lockers are assigned to students. In others, you can choose any locker that has not already been claimed by someone else, and this might be a good reason to get your folks to drive you to school early on the first day.

If you have a choice, take a top locker rather than a bottom one. Seemingly every time a kid with a lower locker kneels to get into it, the slob above him opens his door and unleashes an avalanche of books and papers on the lower kid's head. And

then as he recovers and staggers to his feet, the guy closes his locker and adds a nasty dent to the poor kid's skull.

If your school has lockers without a built-in lock, you will have to bring a lock from home. Pay attention when you are told what kind of lock to bring—combination locks seem to be the usual. You'll feel pretty dorky being the only kid with a cheapo key lock hanging from your locker.

Lots of kids end up locking their combination inside their locker and then forgetting the combination. Unfortunately, doing so is expensive because the school janitor then has to cut the lock off with huge snippers for you to get to your combination—which you suddenly will no longer need. You can avoid being typical by writing your combination on your arm. Or you can write it in pencil on your neighbor's locker door like everyone else does.

One of your friends may want to share lockers with you. What is often best for your friendship is for you to refuse. Sharing makes fitting all of your junk and all your friend's junk in one locker tough. Not to mention the fact that you may find your friend uses more of your stuff than just your locker.

picky particulars

As you go from class to class, your teachers will undoubtedly give special instructions. Since your day is going to be so baffling, you probably won't remember anything you are told to do from one class to the next. This is the time to get out your trusty pencil and write down what each teacher tells you. For example, in some classes you'll get books and be told to put covers on them. In other classes you'll be asked to bring certain items with you every day. If you learn to write down the various instructions you are given, you will come to class prepared. That is, as long as you remember to take home the notebook you've made your notes in!

Learn to write down the various instructions you are given.

lonely lunches

Now it is time for lunch. If you go to a large school, you may be surprised to find that there are several lunch times. You may be scheduled to eat during the first lunch while all your friends are assigned to the second lunch period. Don't bother to complain—the bad news is that most school administrators will shed very few tears over the fact that you must eat alone and will not agree to switch your lunch time. Look around and try to make a few new friends.

Pepto-Bismol, please

Have you ever wondered where all the leftover food that you turned your nose up at and told your parents to send to the starving kids in Africa really goes? Well, now you know. It ends up in the school cafeteria.

I don't think anyone who has gone through Middle School has ever actually *liked* school cafeteria food. The rubber chicken, lumpy mashed potatoes and limp salad are eaten strictly to

avoid starvation. If you can't stomach what is served, you can always bring food from home. But you may not want to carry it in same old the lunch box you used in elementary school. Except for those making an anti-fashion statement, lunch boxes are usually considered dumb. You can't go wrong with a standard brown paper bag—it's been the traditional school lunch accessory for years.

notorious teachers

You'll learn things about many of your teachers before you even enter their classrooms. Sometimes students who have just come from a certain class will spread these facts during lunchtime. More often they will come from older kids who have already had a certain teacher.

Try to keep an open mind about all your teachers. Some are labeled *crummy* or *mean* by the featherheads who want to goof off and aren't able to get away with it. You may really enjoy a teacher that everybody else dislikes.

unearned reputations

If you have older brothers or sisters, you may be pegged before you even get to school. Obviously, this isn't fair. But if your sister was a math whiz and you can't add four to four without a calculator, be prepared to hear your math teacher say, "Well, Junior, it's going to be great having another brilliant student from the Jones family." And try not to gag.

The situation is even worse if you have an older brother or sister who was a troublemaker. Being sent to the vice principal's office every day, simply because you share your family's name with a big brother or sister who is a jerk, is humiliating.

naked kids

A major fear of many new Middle School kids is the need to get undressed and take group showers in Physical Education. (Many Middle Schools require their students to change into gym clothes for P.E. and to shower afterward.) If this fear has haunted you, it may be about to become a reality. Most schools do not have private dressing rooms. In fact, you may feel like a steer as you are herded through the shower stalls.

Expect to be very uncomfortable at first—not only with your own body, but also with the fact that, unless you were raised in a nudist colony, you have never seen so many naked people before in your life.

Some kids try to put off the inevitable by wearing their P.E. uniforms under their school clothes, by refusing to suit up for class, or by skipping showers (thereby blessing everyone who gets too close with the sour smell of body odor.) Even though you may not be happy about the communal showering, this is another change you will have to swallow hard and accept. In a couple of weeks it won't seem so bad.

one last word

Well, we've covered most of the experiences that you will encounter on the first day. The one thing that you probably won't experience—and you may have feared it—is getting into an argument with some other kid. Take heart. On the first day, even school bullies are too busy getting lost to spend much time picking on other kids. Give them a day or two to adjust and then they'll come around to pick on you.

surviving
middle school
chapter two

everybody is looking at me!

*J*ohn was a smiling and likeable kid. He had thick, curly hair, a square head connected to a pudgy body, and two false front teeth. John took great pleasure in clicking those teeth out at girls to make them groan and scream. He seemed to have only two or three shirts, and his shoelaces were always untied. John sat in front of me during social studies, and he was my friend.

But that didn't stop me from secretly taping a sign that read, "KICK ME" to his back. For an entire morning, good ol'

John dodged flying feet. Suddenly the center of attention, he had all the other kids coming up to him, telling him, "Okay!" and hauling off with a swift kick.

The fun ended in math class when John trudged through a gauntlet of extended feet and the teacher, instead of granting the wish taped to his back, removed it. Naturally, everyone thought the joke was quite funny. That is, everyone except John!

But failing to see the humor in his situation didn't stop him from trying the same stunt on a kid who sat in front of him in English.

For a short while, John was the joke of the school, a fate that most of us fear. Wanting to be liked and accepted is natural. No one wants to be thought of as bizarre—unless being bizarre is the only way to get attention. We want to be thought of as someone that others want to know. In fact, your desire to be liked and accepted is stronger now than it will be at any other period in your life.

sticks and stones

Unfortunately, many of your Middle School "friends" will be extremely cutting and cruel—all in fun, of course. Something you do, say, or even look like will be enough to set them howling for days or to brand you with a nickname impossible to shake. In most circumstances the only options you'll have will be to change friends, become a hermit, or bravely take the jibes with a forced smile. To blubber and cry or to explode in anger will only make you more fun to tease. People love a reaction.

Most of the time the people who like you will be the ones who take advantage of your slipups. One kid in our youth group was named Mike—that is, everyone *called* him Mike until he fell asleep once on a long car trip. Because of his allergies, Mike had developed a habit of sleeping with his mouth open—which wasn't a problem at home in his own bed. But this time he had an audience—and to make things worse, he started to drool. He drooled down his chin, along his neck, and all over the side of the car seat. The scene prompted loud hoots and howls of laughter from all his pals in the car. He was immediately christened "Drool-bucket." The name stuck all the way through high school. I like to imagine the look that crossed some father's face when his daughter told him that she was going to the prom with Drool-bucket.

> **Your desire to be liked and accepted is stronger now than it will be at any other period in your life.**

15

Another seventh grader in this same group had hands with long, bony fingers. After examining them, one of his friends decided that they looked like monkey hands. So the kid—whose real name even *I* can't remember—was nicknamed "Cheetah" after the chimp in the old Tarzan movies. I believe he is still called by that name.

I don't want to alarm you, but if you have a large nose, freckles, eyes of two different colors, webbed toes or an outie bellybutton, you're in for some comments. The most likely kind of comments are the blatantly obvious: "Hey, did you know you have a big nose?" or "How'd you get so many freckles?" and similar brilliant questions or comments. If you're clever, you can always think up some snappy comebacks and have them ready for instant use. For example, if someone asks, "How'd you get so many freckles?" You can smartly rely, "I was getting a sun tan under a screen door. How'd you think?"

I have a friend with a crooked nose—and he's fond of saying, "My nose points north-by-northwest. When people tell me to 'follow my nose', I go in a big circle." He's learned to handle the comments he receives about his, ummm, off-kilter schnozzle.

name games

> **Kids love to twist other people's names into millions of variations.**

If there's nothing too unusual about your looks, the gang may have some fun with your name. Kids love to twist other people's names into millions of variations. You're in real trouble if your name can take on some kind of meaning. In our school we had a film about child molesters. The villain's name was Ralph. Pity the poor kid who also bore that name! When fellow students saw him coming, they would shout in mock terror, "Eeek! It's *Ralph!* Run away! Run away!"

There was one kid who never got direct comments on his last name, even though it was a classic. His name was Brian Butt. *No kidding!* (I am using his real name in this case.) He was huge—twice as big as anyone else in the class (which, of course, explains why no one made fun of him to his face).

Being picked on is part of life, and you've got to learn to take some abuse. I realize that sometimes what people say hurts. Jokes can get old in a hurry and some guys just don't know when to stop giving others a hard time. But the truth is, the fact that you drool in your sleep, have a crooked nose, or have Mooselips for a last name does not make you a winner or a loser. That is decided by the kind of person you are on the inside.

teaming up

You may find yourself in a situation that is tougher to deal with than having people make fun of your name or your kite-sized ears. One of these situations often comes up in P.E. class. Coaches frequently choose team captains and then let these jocks choose their teammates. What this means is that some punk is going to decide whether or not you will be the last player chosen—a humiliating experience. Only those who have been picked last really understand the feeling of rejection this creates.

If you are ever chosen last or if you are usually chosen last, you'll have to decide how to respond. You can let the people who don't think much of your athletic ability make you feel like a failure, but you'll miss a whole bunch of great things about yourself. Perhaps you do other things better than kick footballs. Possibly you will be the one who gets good grades in algebra or who blazes away on a musical instrument few others can play. The fact that you aren't athletic is minor in comparison! Try to avoid feeling bitter toward those who make you feel unwanted. And by all means, avoid using your science class to build bombs for their locker!

> **Like many other things in life, you can't control what others do to you, but you can control what you do to others.**

Like many other things in life, you can't control what others do to you, but you can control what you do to others. If you're reading this book and have never been picked last for a team, you have a great opportunity to make someone else's day a bit better. Try going up to your team captain as he or she is choosing players and suggest not leaving "Ol' Butterfingers" for the last this time. Unless your team leader is a complete peanuthead, he or she may go for your idea. Even if you think they won't, it's worth trying. The smile and surprise you'll see on the poor klutz's face will stay with you a lifetime.

fleeting childhood

Many kids struggle with the feeling that they must give up all the fun stuff and toys of childhood or risk having their friends make rude jokes about them or call them babies.

It's true that as we become adults we leave behind childish things—but hey, you're still a kid! All that's happening is that you're moving on to a more sophisticated level of play.

Sooner or later you you'll have to put the toys of your past behind you, but it's okay to feel sad about that. You're mourning a passage from one stage of life to another. And don't be in a big hurry to stop messing around with what other kids may label as "toys." Play with your stuff at home, in private, and nobody will give you a hard time. You'll be grown up for most of your life, so enjoy being a kid while you can.

a healthy self-image

Experiences in Middle School can shake your self-confidence and make you wish you were someone else. You may become discouraged about your looks, your athletic ability or your lack of popularity. You may wish for money to buy the clothes or goodies that some other kids seem to have in abundance. Or perhaps you'll feel embarrassed about your parents and wonder if there's any place where you can trade them in for a new, more understanding set. And you even may not be too happy with the real you.

God created you to be great!

If you're having these feelings, please consider the fact that God doesn't make junk. When God made you, He didn't misread the ingredient list or throw in the ugly stick. He made you purposefully—*yes, crooked nose and all!* In fact, God created you to be more than a mediocre, semi-dull, average, middle-class person. He created you to be great!

Great? Yeah, but not in the same way that rock stars and famous politicians are great. He created you to be great in *His* way. Jesus often said things like, "Whoever wants to become great among you must serve the rest of you like a servant." (Matthew 20:26). He repeated Himself a number of times— explaining to people how they could be important in their homes, their schools, and their work situations by being last and being a servant of everyone.

Many people have a hard time making sense of Jesus' words. They sometimes sound like hocus-pocus nonsense. G.K. Chesterton, a famous writer, put Christ's teaching into less puzzling words. He wrote, "The great man is the one who makes every man feel great." This is important for you to understand—especially if you sometimes feel like a bug splat on the windshield of life. To be popular and likeable, you must forget about pleasing yourself and instead work on making other people feel important and likeable.

Forget about pleasing yourself— work on making other people feel important and likeable.

Let me give you an example of how this works. Suppose you and a bunch of your friends are talking about what a wizard you all are on snowboards. In turn, almost all of the kids are describing the great moves they've made, the amount of air they've got or the massive wipeouts they've survived. In a way, you're a bunch of braggarts trying to outdo each other with bigger and better stories and hoping that someone is listening and being impressed.

To make someone else feel great in this situation, make a true but positive comment about the snowboarding ability of a beginner in the group. It's a gift—a free, up-lifting note in a bull session. You'll be amazed at what it will do to warm the heart of your beginner friend. And in turn the friend you have complimented will see you in a slightly new, slightly more valuable light. You have started to become great in the eyes of this friend.

one last word

What Jesus said is true. The way to become great is to stop feeling sorry for yourself or wishing to be somebody else; then start giving kindness and attention to others. With just a moment's reflection, you'll see how this works in your own life. Think for a second about the adults who mean the most to you right now. They are probably the ones who pay attention to you or give you encouragement. They may be your parents, a teacher, the coach, your youthworker or a minister. But you like them for one simple reason: they like you and when you are around them they make you feel great.

You can do the same for a friend.

surviving middle school

chapter three

your mutating body

*J*osh landed in Boys' Choir—which was certainly NOT his first choice. He would have preferred to be in Art, Robotics, Woodshop—any class but Choir. Unfortunately, all those other classes were filled and Josh was told that he would have to wait until the end of the semester for a transfer. So, for the time being, he was in Boys' Choir. But Josh was not alone. Boys' Choir was the dumping ground for all the overloaded elective courses at his particular Middle School.

His teacher was a plump, highly emotional woman named Mrs. Hutton. I don't know how much this woman was paid to lead Boys' Choir, but it couldn't have been enough. Trying to control a bunch of unwilling recruits and getting something that could pass for music from their foul lips was a job deserving of combat pay.

During the first week of school, Mrs. Hutton tested the boys' voices to find out where they would fit into her master plan for turning her rabble into a musical miracle. Josh was forced to sing a short solo. Red-faced, he quietly breathed out his lines in a lofty sweet soprano voice (...uh, for those of you without a drop of musical knowledge, "soprano" is the highest "girly voice" end of the musical range). But weird events were in store for Josh and his friends.

As Josh tried to hit some of the notes in the songs the choir was practicing, his voice would crack without warning and tumble from lilting heights to some lower depths that sounded harsh and tuneless. Josh's voice was changing. By the time Josh was able to transfer to a shop class, he was singing in the baritone section of the choir. His voice had dropped two octaves in a few months. So common was this situation that Mrs. Hutton's soprano section was down to a couple of kids by the end of the year.

an era of changes

Welcome to the time of life when your body does whatever it wants, whenever it wants—without notifying you! Have you ever watched an old Wolfman movie? The sweet lovable guy turns into a hairy monster when the moon is full. Well, that is kind of what's happening to you, only you are changing a bit more slowly, with or without the full moon—and with any luck you will not end up quite so hairy.

Everybody experiences this mutation; nobody gets left out.

You are changing in body from a kid to an adult; it's mutating from a familiar freckle-faced, goofy-looking twerp into something yet unknown. Although you may not notice how quickly this is happening, you can be sure that Aunt Bertha will comment on it at the next family gathering.

There are a few facts that you should realize about this time of change. First of all, please keep in mind that sooner or later everybody experiences this mutation; nobody gets left out. No matter how skinny, flat, hairless, short or baby-faced you are, dramatic changes are on the way.

But the next fact is just as important: bodies change at different speeds. Some kids you know will be huge hairy monsters or shapely beauties by the seventh grade. And you may even find yourself part of this group. Others will change very little. You may have guessed that some kids who are late bloomers are self-conscious about being small and hairless, but you may be surprised to learn that many of those who develop early feel just as weird. They fail to see their early development as a good thing because it makes them different from other kids.

And did you know that bodies often develop or grow unevenly? For example, a boy's legs may grow so quickly and out of proportion with the rest of his body that he becomes clumsy. A girl may find that one breast grows a little faster than the other one, or that she grows everywhere but her bust line.

Relax. Things will sort themselves out eventually.

Physical changes often affect your eating habits. You may develop a huge appetite and feel hungry all of the time. Remember, you're try-ing to feed a mutating body. If you find that your stomach insists on growling in class and demanding food, get in the habit of car-rying extra fruit or cheese in your lunch to use for snacks.

Sometimes a growth spurt will cause pain in your arms, legs, elbows or knees. These experiences are normal but uncomfort-able. Be comforted by the thought that they will eventually go away and leave you with a mature physique.

measures of maturity

Just because a kid happens to look older than everyone else in his or her class does not mean that he or she is more mature. Maturity is far more a measure of what is on the inside than it is a measure of what is on the outside. And though you may be tempted to envy those kids in grown-up bodies, developing early is not always best for you in the long run.

Tami was already developing curves in elementary school. By the time she hit eighth grade she looked like a young woman, not a kid in Middle School. Other girls envied her. Boys would whisper their thoughts about her body to each other as she passed by.

But because she looked older, Tami attracted older boys – boys who drove cars rather than rode skateboards or bikes. Tami was fascinated by their attention, and they were taken with her gorgeous body. Before long, Tami was pregnant. Because her parents were Christians, they decided that she should not have an abortion. Tami dropped out of school until the baby was born. Then she put the child up for adoption and transferred to another school district.

Developing early is not always best for you.

Tami's physical maturity caused problems because she appeared older on the outside than she really was on the inside. The sex vultures in any community spot these early bloomers in a hurry and are quick to devour them!

Jason's case was not so tragic. He simply reached physical maturity before anyone else. By eighth grade he could grow a full beard—much to the envy of the other guys who would have ruptured themselves trying to squeeze one shavable hair from their chins. But often those who get it first, lose it first.

No, Jason didn't lose the hair on his face. That stayed nice and healthy. But Jason was bald by the time he was twenty-one!

And Tami, the curvy eighth grader? She was in her prime during Middle School and from then on her life was all downhill. The funny thing is that all those thin, flat, scrawny, underdeveloped boys and girls who are not much to look at in Middle School often blossom suddenly in high school—much to everyone's delight.

If you are an early bloomer, your situation is far from hopeless. I've told two stories that may leave you a bit concerned. Take heart! Kids who physically mature early do not always find themselves in crummy situations. In fact, during Middle School you can take advantage—in a good way—of being bigger or more developed than almost everyone else. Here are a couple of suggestions.

- *Get Involved in Sports.* This is your chance to be a real superstar. You can probably outrun, outjump and outswim most of the little squirts you compete against. Being involved in sports is also a good way to expend energy and stay out of trouble.

- *Develop Leadership Skills.* Curiously, in Middle School many kids tend to look up to somebody they, uh, *have* to "look up" to. This is a chance to be a leader, not a follower. Since the school bully will seldom want to tangle with someone who is bigger than he is, you have a chance to be a hero—you can become a "bodyguard" for smaller friends who may be getting picked on!

Even though your body may be looking more mature, you shouldn't stop acting your age. Avoid the pressure to "be as grown up as you look." Enjoy being a kid—you won't get to be one again!

changing emotions

Most girls have their first menstrual period during Middle School. Your body can take a while to fall into a regular twenty-eight-day cycle. To avoid any unpleasant accidents, always carry an extra pad or tampon in your purse or backpack in case your period decides to surprise you and start up during school. These periods may also create some discomfort, grouchiness, and lack of energy. Be sensitive to your body's need for more rest and realize that this is not a good time to be making important decisions. And if one of your friends acts unusually moody, try not to take her too seriously. She'll probably be a new person in a few days.

smelly subject

And now for a bit of bad news. Very soon, if not already, your body is going to start stinking. Yeah, I'm talking about serious B.O. and foot rot. In every Middle School group there is one kid who still hasn't gotten the message about using deodorant and taking daily showers. His teeth are green from yesterday's lunch, his feet smell as though they've been dead inside his shoes for a month, and visible fumes seep out from under his arms. The only kids who will sit next to him are the ones with such bad head colds that they can't notice the foul aroma swirling around them.

You see, when you were a little kid, you could sweat up a storm and at the worst smell slightly stale. But as the changes that move you toward adulthood begin, "stale" is replaced with "stink." This is where good *hygiene* (cleanliness) comes in. You're going to have to shower and wash thoroughly (with soap), use B.O. juice (deodorant), brush and floss your teeth, and change your socks and underwear *every day*. Otherwise, you'll get a label that you don't want. And besides, you'll find that talking others into allowing you in a crowded car is much easier if you smell decent.

This is where good hygiene (cleanliness) comes in.

Another little pleasure that some kids experience is dandruff. You've seen people with snowstorms of flakes on their shoulders. It's gross *and* avoidable. The solution? Wash your hair every day. If you scalp tends to be flaky, use a dandruff shampoo. Unless you have some special skin problem, daily washing should take care of any flakiness.

blemish blues

Probably the worst plague you may face will be the sudden emergence of zits. A clear, sweet face can look like a battlefield with eyeballs overnight. Blackheads, pimples, and zits are caused by the sudden increase of oils in and on your skin. When oils, dirt and grime collect on your face, find their way into your pores and clog them, they create blackheads. When pores get infected or irritated, they turn into gnarly and sometimes painful pimples. Zits are somewhat related to what you eat (oily foods and chocolate), but they are usually controllable by scrubbing your face with soap, water, and a washcloth.

Some people consider pimples to be the end of the world. They are sure that everyone notices the nasty things. The truth is that unless a zit is the size of Mount Everest, it probably won't be noticed at all. But people *will* notice if you take such lousy care of your skin that you get a zit farm going. If you find a zit on your face, don't pick at it, especially if your fingers are dirty. It will only make the rotten thing look like Mount St. Helens has erupted on your face and possibly cause a more serious infection. Obviously, if you have a big white ball of pus hanging from the end of your nose, you've got to get rid of it. Just make sure that you sanitize anything that will touch your face. Rubbing alcohol works well. Think of yourself as a doctor doing minor surgery.

Acne is another nasty complexion problem that may affect you as you move through your changes. This skin condition looks a lot like zits gone wild. It can spread from your face to your back and is hard to control. If your parents struggled with acne, you have a greater chance of getting it too. Although some people have trouble with acne in their twenties or during a pregnancy, most people find that it is at its worst during their teenage years.

People WILL notice if you take lousy care of your skin.

Acne is very difficult to control without help. Naturally, keeping your face clean helps; but if you think you're getting acne, you may need to see a special skin doctor known as a dermatologist. Dermatologists can prescribe special medicines and treatments to help control acne. Severe cases can scar your face for life, so don't mess around. See a doctor.

brace face

By this point in life, most kids have lost their baby teeth and have their permanent ones. And a lot of time the permanent teeth are crooked. For this reason, you'll see a lot of kids with braces on their teeth in Middle School.

If you're afflicted with braces, you may feel very ashamed of your appearance and may try to smile without showing your teeth. Don't bother. Braces are so common that most kids won't even notice whether you are wearing them or not. In fact, some kids just go all the way and order braces with bright coloring just for the fun of it. Thank your folks for spending loads of money so that you can have a nice smile—and keep away from strong magnets.

the opposite sex

Of all the changes you'll experience during Middle School, none will be so noticeable to you as the changes you experience sexually. As you transmogrify from child to adult, you may be shocked to discover hair growing in some very private places. Boys sometimes experience *wet dreams* at night (when your penis ejaculates semen) or erections at embarrassing moments. Girls, who are often a little ahead of boys at this stage of development, may find themselves daydreaming about getting married to some kid in school or about attracting male attention.

When you were a little kid, you probably thought that the opposite sex had cooties, was stupid or was a waste of time. You might have been curious about what the other sex looks like under all those clothes, but it never interested you as it may right now in Middle School.

I'll tell you more about what you can expect from these feelings in another chapter, but I need to say this here: the fascination you may feel toward a member of the opposite sex is normal. It's like hunger. There is a time and place for it—just as mealtime is the time and place for satisfying the hunger for food. God tells us that we need to control our sexual urges until the time is right. And God knows what He is talking about!

There's no such thing as "normal" — everyone is abnormal at this time of life!

Again, because we all develop at varying speeds, don't feel that you are weird if you don't experience any of what I've just described until you hit high school. There's no such thing as normal—everyone is abnormal at this time of life!

All in all, the changes that you go through physically during your Middle School years are amazing. You may outgrow your clothes every few months, discover new emotions and feelings, and be astonished that you look so little like a kid and so much like an adult. But there is one thing you can be sure of: God didn't make a mistake when He made you. He hasn't forgotten you, nor has He played a dirty trick on you. You will not mutate into an alien or some kind of huge toad. You will slowly become a mature man or woman.

So relax and enjoy the process. Be yourself, even if you find that your body is maturing more slowly or more quickly than you would like. In other words, forget the padded bra!

safety first

Keep in mind that you get only one body in this life and that it's your job to take care of it. If you are reckless on your bike or skateboard, you will leave large amounts of skin on the sidewalk. Take precautions and throw on some safety gear. Don't think that you are made out of rubber—because you are not! Be a little cautious—the life you risk is your own.

Don't do stuff like tattooing or intentionally scarring your body. You will likely regret it later in life. (Even guys who get professionally tattooed in their adult life will tell you not to do it in Middle School.) Don't experiment with things obviously harmful to your body—things like drugs, alcohol and tobacco. Remember that every smoker who dies of lung cancer started out thinking that he or she would beat the odds—and didn't. What I'm trying to tell you is to do the best you can to keep your body and mind in good shape, and God will do His best to make sure you end up with a final product that both of you will be happy with.

one last word

Here's a word of wisdom that comes from my mother. She told me when I was a growing kid:

> **"The only thing you should stick in your ear—is your elbow."**

surviving middle school
chapter four

the campus zoo

*I*n some ways going to Middle School is like going to the zoo because a whole collection of different species exists on campus. Each one has its own gathering place: one crew dominates the steps; another congregates in the north corner of the field; another group meets under the big tree. And just like the critters at the zoo, they leave their marks behind: soda cans and candy wrappers litter some sites, names carved in wood, scratched in stone or dug out of grass are found in others, and cigarette butts still smolder on the ground at the far end of the campus.

Often each group will dress and talk differently from all the others. If you don't look and talk like the kids in a particular group, you won't be allowed to hang out with them. In fact, they will consider you to be at the same level as a maggot.

These groups also dominate different areas of the cafeteria or lunch court during feeding time. Pity the poor kid from one species who tries to eat in another's territory. At the least, stares and growls will make it clear that he or she is not welcome.

A whole collection of different species exists on campus.

Most of these little clusters have a ringleader, a small group of disciples ("*toadies*") who find pleasure in serving the ringleader, and varying numbers of fringe members ("*wannabes*"). Just as in the animal kingdom, the ringleader is most often the largest or most physically mature kid in the group.

If you don't belong to a group, you will feel pressured to find a group with which to hang out. This is natural and really very important because we all need to feel that we fit in and are liked.

Almost every Middle School houses the same *kinds* of species. Hairstyles, slang words, music and fashion may change from campus to campus, but the nature of the groups remains the same. Use the following species list to prepare yourself for what you will find on your campus. Your school may not have all of these groups and subgroups, but it will have many of them and maybe some others I haven't mentioned. Species may even mutate before this book comes off the press!

bullies

This is the most feared species by those entering Middle School. Although Bullies do prowl the halls and playgrounds of Middle School, they are usually of little threat to new students—unless a newcomer accidentally trips one! Usually Bullies are bigger, meaner and nastier than the rest of the student population. Bullies are also dumber and think they are cooler because they can beat up on everyone else. People may fear bullies, but few people like them.

HURT, KILL, MAIM, DUH...

The best way to deal with Bullies is to avoid them. Walk the other way and don't make snide comments or give them any reason to show you who's the boss. If walking away from tense situations is difficult for you, make friends with someone who will come to your rescue when you're picked on. Most big goons don't want to mess with those who might take them down in a fight.

I know that in your wildest fantasies you might think you are able to stand up to a mean, drooling, wart-faced Bully and beat him into a pancake. But unless you have a black-belt in some martial art, just remember that your thoughts are fantasy!

Strangely enough, sometimes even small-but-tough kids will start acting like Bullies, just to make up for their size. These kids have to choose their victims carefully or their life expectancies will be shorter than they are!

girl bullies

Your rules for dealing with male Bullies also apply to female ones.

In some schools you will find a few girls that go around acting tough and picking fights with other girls. For most kids in Middle School, watching a fight is highly entertaining and watching a couple of girls fight is better than watching the Superbowl. (This is probably because girls fight dirty: pulling hair, scratching, biting as well as hitting.) Your rules for dealing with male Bullies also apply to female ones: ignore them and don't allow yourself to be pushed into a fight.

jock and jockettes

This group is made up of sports freaks. They usually love baseball, football, soccer, volleyball, and basketball—just about any sport in which players run around and get sweaty. Often this group has many of the larger students in the school, and Jocks are rarely pushed around or hassled. They also have lots of photos of themselves in the school yearbook.

You might assume that Jockettes are girls that play sports, but not all of them do; they are just as likely to be the girls who hang around with Jocks. Many of them are cheerleaders (or future High School cheerleaders) and are very pretty—but they won't give you the time of day unless you are a Jock.

substrata athletes

This species can be found in almost every school. They are the kids who participate in sports not sponsored or recognized by the school, but recognized by everyone else. Sometimes substrata athletes—and the girls who hang out with them or participate in the same sports—are even more popular than the Jocks and Jockettes.

Substrata sports are often determined by region. Schools near the ocean will have surfers and body boarders who lick the salt off themselves in first period. In mountainous areas

you'll find snowboarders and skiers hanging out together and discussing their most daring feats. In other schools you may find cowpokes wearing boots, hats and monstrous belt buckles to school. These boys are happiest when wresting bulls to the ground. Almost every school has skateboarders creating havoc on whatever concrete they can find and bleeding on their desks from unhealed road rash. Most schools have online gamers who geek together at weekend LAN parties. And no doubt, at a school in some remote corner of the globe, a group of walrus hunters or trapeze artists hang out together.

party animals

Even in Middle School you may find these creatures. They live to "party"—which usually means drinking booze until they throw up, or experimenting with various kinds of drugs, or looking around for someone to make out with.

Much of what party animals talk about is pure fiction, but some really do have access to alcohol and drugs through older friends, brothers, sisters and, sometimes, even parents. Needless to say, hanging out with this crowd is a bad idea, even though the kids in this group seem carefree and fun-loving. The fire they are playing with is deadly.

fashion models

These girls spend all of their time leafing through fashion magazines, going to the mall to endlessly try on outfits, and putting on make up. They begin shaving their legs before they have hair on them and are already saving their allowance for some kind of plastic surgery so they can have the "perfect" nose, butt, chin or chest. Some of them even refuse to suit up for gym class because they are afraid of messing up their hair.

Except for the fact that their bodies are underdeveloped, these girls dress and look a lot older than they really are. Unfortunately, the ability to look older doesn't make a person more mature. Still, they put on a good act.

The male version of this species is rare in Middle School, but sometimes is found in High School. They are called "Metrosexuals" or "G.Q.ers" (after a fashion magazine created for men). You'll find them under the "best dressed" section in the yearbook.

burnouts

These are the kids who have really had to struggle to get as far as sixth grade. They show up for school when the wind blows the right direction, and they seem to come from homes where no one knows who or where they are.

Burnouts never do their homework, have lost their schoolbooks, and are just putting in time until they can flunk out of school completely. Many burnouts have been to "juvy" (juvenile hall) as more than visitors. They often cloud the bathroom with smoke and refuse to suit up for P.E.

clowns

Although this species does not technically group together, these individuals are found in every class or group. Clowns often can be persuaded to do things that normal people would never do: wash their hair in toilets, spill marbles in the hall during class break, eat bugs—anything, just to get some laughs.

Clowns are quite fun to have around as long as they know when to quit—which, unfortunately, is a skill they usually lack.

freaks

Freaks are the kids in any Middle School that favor giving adults a shock treatment. They play at full volume the noisiest and most obscene music possible, or enjoy quoting the worst of the lyrics as if they were poetry. Sometimes they wear clothes that are obviously designed to be outrageous or to have gory, macabre or bizarre images that (hopefully) will cause parents to worry that these kids have gone over to the dark side.

Freaks vary from school to school and change shocking devices from time to time. But the same basic species is easy to spot.

brains

Really smart kids often hang out together.

You probably know who fits in this category. Yep! It's those kids born with computer chips in place of actual brains. Really smart kids often hang out together; either because no other group wants them around or because no one else has a vocabulary large enough to understand them. The funny thing is that most average kids distance themselves from the brain group only until they need help on the big quiz in English.

sex fiends

This strange kid is a subspecies of various species. Almost always a boy, the Sex Fiend talks or jokes about sex, body parts, and girls endlessly. A giant walking hormone, this kind of boy rarely has a real girlfriend. Instead he spends his spare time downloading pictures of naked women (this is called pornography) to his phone, computer and any other device that can hold an image.

His fascination with sex causes him to limit his friendship to those who don't mind a constant bombardment of sexual talk. He doesn't even mind being branded as the "Perv-guy." What this kid really needs is to get involved in an active sport and to take a nice cold shower.

floaters

Most likely you'll start Middle School as a Floater. Floaters don't really have to identify with a particular group. Instead they move freely between groups. Floaters generally feel a little bit left out because they are not firm members of any species on campus. At the same time, most Floaters are happy to have a large number of acquaintances and friends that moving between groups offers.

outcasts

Remember reading in the Bible about the people who contracted leprosy and had to stay away from the general

population for fear they would give the disease to others? Well, there usually are a few kids on campus who fit into this category. Most of the time these kids do not band together as a group but rather remain lonely and friendless.

The reasons for their sad plight are numerous. Sometimes it's because they look, smell or dress oddly, and sometimes it's because of all three. Sometimes they have poor social skills and have difficulty making friends. Sometimes they act a bit peculiar or say strange things (think "Napoleon Dynamite").

Most of the time there is little that outcasts can do to break into a group. Instead, they become the target of all of those cowardly enough to make jokes at their expense.

homeboys and honkies

In some schools you will find that certain kids hang out with other kids of a similar race or culture. Sometimes these groups dress, carry themselves and talk in a particular way. Often they listen to a certain kind of music. Among themselves, they will make rude racial jokes or comment about others who are not like them.

Naturally this kind of grouping does very little to help ease tension and hostility. These kids can come off strong and pushy—as long as they have their gang to back them up. Transfer these guys to schools where they cannot hang out with others of their race or culture, and they become timid in a hurry.

choosing your group

In your Middle School you can probably identify a number of species that I haven't even mentioned in this chapter. The important thing to remember is to be wise in picking the species you want to hang out with and to avoid thinking that your group is better than any other.

> **Be wise in picking the species you want to hang out with.**

When you're ready to pick or locate the group you want to hang out with, follow a few tips:

- *Hang out with winners and you'll become a winner.* If you hang out with losers, you'll become a loser. In other words—take a long, hard look at the people in the group that you would like to be a part of. Make sure that they are the kind of people you really want to be like and that they are not into doing things you know are wrong or unhealthy for you physically or spiritually.

- *You will tend to become like those you spend time with.* This issue can have a great effect on who you become. For example, if you struggle a bit getting decent grades, it would be dumb (although admittedly comfortable) to hang out with people who ditch classes or do poorly in school. Those friends won't build you up; they will bring you down to their level. In contrast, if you hang out with people who do well in school, you will find that your grades improve as well.

- *Don't join just any group that will accept you.* You don't need to be desperate. Some groups will take anyone who does what is required by the group. Be selective enough to hang out with the kind of people you really like and don't have to be ashamed of.

- *Be careful about putting down other groups or species on campus.* This kind of behavior may be fun (laughing at someone else's strangeness usually is), but it leads to a snotty attitude and a very nasty condition called "pride."

one last word

Finding a good group of friends to hang out with can be one of the most important turning points in your life. Finding the wrong species of friends to hook up with can be one of the worst.

Be wise.

surviving middle school
chapter five

making up your own mind

*A*nswer these questions honestly:

- How would you feel if your mom selected your school clothes for you each day?

- What would you do if your friends canceled your order at the Golden Arches and ordered what *they* wanted you to eat instead?

- How would you react if someone told you what music to listen to and what music is junk?

I think I know how you would feel and what you would say: "I can make up my own mind!" And you would very likely be right. Unless you are color blind, can't read a menu, or have an X-rated taste in music, you are probably able to make these decisions yourself. You've come to a point in life when you will have to make up your own mind about things—not only about what to wear to school, what to eat, and what to listen to, but also about many other important issues in life.

peer pressure

The most frequent response I hear from my Middle School friends when the subject of peer pressure comes up is, "I don't let anybody tell me what to do. I make my own decisions!" Maybe so. But living in this world, we will far more likely find ourselves bending with the influences of society and especially our friends.

During one experiment on the power of peer pressure, several students were placed in a room with a projector and a huge screen. On the screen was an image of three numbered lines, two of similar length and one obviously of greater length. The researchers gave the group a moment to study the lines, then turned off the projector and asked the individuals in the group to identify which line was the longest.

Sound easy, huh? Well, there was a catch. All of the participants except one had been privately instructed to select the line that was not the shortest, but obviously not the longest. When the researchers asked the

group to give their choices, all except the unknowing participant voted for the *wrong* line. Seeing that the group outnumbered him, the individual who *knew* the right answer changed his mind, decided that he was mistaken and voted for the wrong answer.

The researchers conducted the experiment a number of times with different groups. On each occasion, the student who actually knew the right answer voted with the majority anyway. This is an example of classic peer pressure: to go against what you know to be true and right in order to be in step with the rest of the group.

critical choices

Of course, going along with the crowd's decision on the length of a line is no big deal; but going along with them on other concerns, like hurting other people or going against our own convictions, makes a whole world of difference.

When you start making your own decisions you need to know that people are prone to become clones. In other words, your friends and society mold you a whole lot more than you realize. Think about it. Do you like the same style of music your friends like? Do you favor the same sports or activities? Do you dress in the same style? Do you use the same slang phrases, tell the same jokes, use the same words? "Well sure," you say, "but having these things in common is what made us friends." That's possible, but it's more likely that because you are friends, you have become like each other.

You can see this process at work on your school campus. Imagine a kid starts hanging out with some guys who speak pig Latin, shave polka dots out of their hair, and howl at the moon. It'll be just a matter of time before this normal kid becomes a moon-howling, polka-dot-headed, pig-Latin-chirping member of the tribe.

be choosy

Because our friends influence us, we must try to pick quality people for our friends. In the experiment I shared with you earlier, when the researchers tried the routine with *two* uninformed participants instead of one, the pair banded together and insisted that they were right and everyone else was wrong. And of course, they were correct. The Bible advises, "Bad friends will ruin good habits." (1 Corinthians 15:33)

We need to acknowledge that we *do* want to be like our friends. We don't want to be outcasts. We're afraid that if we resist the flow of the group too much we will be kicked out of the club. The independence we claim so proudly often goes only as far as our group allows.

Some people will go to almost any length to be part of the crowd. Jeff, a kid in my youth group, is one of those guys—a nice kid, but a wannabe follower of whatever group would accept him. He had a wishbone for a backbone.

One warm summer afternoon, Jeff and a few of his friends took to the back roads of their small town. Quite suddenly, they came upon the carcass of a large toad. Now this toad had been dead for a number of days and had been flattened into a Frisbee by passing cars. It was in lousy shape.

After a number of gross jokes, some in the group dared Jeff to eat the toad. When Jeff balked, the pressure increased. Accusations of cowardice were added and triple-dog-dare-ya's were heaved onto the pile. Finally, the demands to eat the toad were reduced to merely taking a bite out of it. Jeff reached down, picked up the dried toad, bit off the crispy little head and immediately spit it into the bushes. The group howled in laughter and groaned in disgust. Soon Jeff's actions were legendary. He was offered the honor of being the school Grock. (In case you don't know, the definition of a Grock is "one who bites off the heads of animals in public.")

Jeff wanted to please his friends so much that he did the unthinkable to win their approval. Although most of us would stop short of chomping on dead toads to avoid being outcasts, we may be willing to do a whole bundle of other things. To understand and acknowledge this tendency is the first step toward truly being able to make up our own minds.

In a Middle School setting you will probably have opportunity to see, hear and do a lot of things that would never have been part of your elementary school experience. Swings and sandboxes are out. Being cool is in. Some of these ideas and activities will have to do with the things your friends enjoy. Some of the ideas and activities will be passed along through the school and through the teachers themselves. For every bit of information you receive, for every action you are invited to take part in, you will be expected to make up our own mind—or have someone else make it up for you.

> **Make up your own mind— or have someone else make it up for you.**

healthy doubting

You many already have figured out that not everything you read, see, or hear—even from adults—is true or accurate. I remember when this truth first dawned on one of my sons. We were standing in line at the supermarket, waiting to unload the piles of food that were quickly defrosting in our cart. Surrounding us at the check stand were goodies, begging for a chance to come home with us. Included were a number of so-called newspapers with the names like *The National Snoop* and *The Daily Tattletale*.

One of those tabloids caught my son's attention. The headline declared, "Baby from Mars Born to a Human Mother," with a picture of the baby with small antennae protruding from its head. "Dad," he said in a serious tone, "a lady had a baby from Mars."

At this point we had one of those long father-to-son talks about not believing everything you see in print. The concept stunned him. "But how can they print it if it's not true?" he complained. Good question, but beside the point.

If we think for a few minutes, we will be able to see through the idiotic attempts people make to get us to believe that the products they sell will create magic. Take, for example, a mouthwash that promises to give its users sex appeal. Imagine a big, green-toothed, greasy-haired, rumpled, wart-faced junk collector. Do you  imagine for one second that giving this guy a swig of this miraculous mouthwash will suddenly cause him to be overrun with beautiful girls in bikinis? Not a chance.

Ads are created and aired for one reason: they work. There are a whole lot of mental midgets squatting in front of their TV screens who figure that if something is said over the airwaves, it must be true.

And as the old adage goes, "If it seems too good to be true, it probably isn't!" Be somewhat of a skeptic and healthy doubter.

get picky

In Middle School you will be doing a whole lot of picking. You will be picking your friends, your clothes, your music, your sports, your image, and sometimes even your nose (hopefully not in public). You will be making choices. It's an awesome responsibility.

Sometimes you will make the wrong choice. For example, let's suppose that you decide to hang out with Jenny Brown. You think she is nice, friendly and funny. Some of your other friends think she is a creep; your mom dislikes her so much that she wants you to wear a garlic wreath and crucifix around your neck and keep a hammer and wooden stake handy.

The reactions of your mom and friends only push you further into the relationship. You find yourself defending Jenny, even when you begin to have second thoughts about the friendship. As time goes by, you find that every time Jenny visits your house, some of your clothes go home with her *–without your permission*. Naturally, Jenny either denies that she has taken anything or claims that you said she could borrow them.

> **You will be making choices. It's an awesome responsibility.**

Slowly you come to discover that Jenny is not quite the person you thought she was. She has morals and habits that would get you put under house arrest until you are eighteen if you imitated them. Jenny is not the kind of friend that you had hoped she would be. You've made a mistake in judgment, and your mom—in one of her rare moments—was right after all. So you go looking for a wooden stake.

one last word

This is very important: you need to make up your own mind about your relationship with God. If you were raised in a Christian home, most likely you've merely adopted  the values and ideas of your family. Now is the time for you to decide if you truly want to know and walk with God. You can't inherit Christianity in the same way that you inherit brown eyes, curly hair, buckteeth or a crooked nose. Christianity is a *choice*. Your upbringing can help you see the choice more clearly, but cannot make the choice for you.

You'll have to do some hard thinking about what being a follower of Christ really means. Not everyone is willing to do what is required in order to be a true believer. If you have questions or doubts about God or about the Bible, talk to a Christian adult whom you trust. You'll be able to get helpful information that will allow you to make an intelligent choice.

To make up your mind in favor of a relationship with God does not mean that you are going to be perfect. It often means failure. But it is the same kind of failure that you experienced as a baby when you were learning to walk. You didn't give up—you don't crawl to school! Nope, you whipped up a little more determination and pulled yourself up for another try.

True faith is very much like that. In the end, your faith will have to be your own and not anyone else's. It's up to you to make up your mind.

surviving
middle school
chapter six

love and romance –
middle school style

You may be one of those people who will want to skip this chapter. The members of the opposite sex are of no interest to you. In fact, you and your buddies have made a pact promising *never* to like girls. Or maybe you are simply too busy having fun to take notice of the whole boyfriend/girlfriend scene.

No problem! Just come back and read this chapter when ol' Cupid decides to stick you with one of his arrows. You have plenty of time to deal with the subject at hand. Enjoy what interests you now. But if that's not you, please consider some of these thoughts.

secret loves

The vast majority of Middle School romances are one-sided. In other words, one person really likes another person, but never tells that person or tries to get the other person to return the affection. The person who is "in love" often hopes that the other person will simply notice and feel the same way, but the relationship rarely works out.

This is a tough situation for the kid who really wishes to win the affection of a secret love, but most people in this situation choose to keep quiet rather than risk rejection. What I am trying to tell you is that if you get all the way through Middle

School without ever having a true girlfriend or boyfriend, don't worry! You are the average person, not the reject weirdo.

If you are brave enough to try communicating your interest in another person, you will face the problem of how to do so. The usual method is to tell your big-mouthed friends and then sit back and wait for them to spread the news. And believe me, they will! They'll probably go right up to the guy you like and say something direct like, "Hey, did you know that Jenna likes you?"

You can also try calling him or her on the phone, a course of action that can be very scary. After all, what do you say? You have to have a reason to call—at least for the first time. And what if the person you call is really cold on the other end of the phone? What if he or she has their speaker option turned on and you are broadcasting live in front of all his or her friends? What if you get his or her parents?

> **If you must write a love note, use disappearing ink on self-destructing paper.**

When phone calls are not an option, I have seen some brave (or desperate) people write love notes. Bad idea. Never, *ever* write down on paper or on the computer anything you don't want the whole world to know. For certain, somebody will help your love scribbles get the circulation they *don't* deserve. You'll show your love note to some friends, or confide your feelings via an e-mail or instant message—and they, being such good friends, will steal it, copy it and pass it around the whole school. Another awful thing that can happen is that your mom or dad will discover the love note. So—if you *must* write a love note, use disappearing ink on self-destructing paper.

the bad news

Once two people in Middle School discover each other—and as I said, this is not really the average situation—they are faced with a whole bunch of other issues to consider. Most kids in Middle School are not allowed to date (I am defining a *date* as going somewhere alone with your boyfriend or girlfriend). So the couple ends up hanging out together at school, during games, or at church events.

Some of them want so much to be alone that they cram themselves into the "make-out row" in the back of the van or bus, the back rows of the movie theater, or any deep, dark woods they can find. This desire to want to hang out with the person you like so much is very natural, but may cause some problems with your friends.

Kids who get overly involved in romantic relationships will lose ground with their other friends. Their pals will no longer bother to invite them to play football because "lover boy" is too busy with his girlfriend—or even worse, wants to drag her along. (And besides, most of Romeo's friends don't have girlfriends, so they are extremely unsympathetic.) The girls

may be a little more faithful to a friend skewered by Cupid's arrow, but they eventually become jealous and tired of hearing about how great so-and-so is. Having a boyfriend or girlfriend is the pits for your other social life!

Most Middle School romances have short life expectancies. It's rare to find people who have been together for more that six months. Most of the time kids just get bored or a new prospect comes along.

A lot of kids who have partners in Middle School do something called *going together.* This simply means that they are not interested in getting new boyfriends or girlfriends right now—give them a month or two. Some kids get really emotional about going together and exchange rings or necklaces.

> **Most Middle School romances have short life expectancies.**

Things can get very gooey.

parents' reactions

By the way, parents react to the news that their children are "going steady" in different ways. Some go crazy and threaten to shoot their daughter's boyfriend if he comes around; others just smile and say, "That's nice," or "Isn't it cute? Junior has found himself a little girlfriend!" Besides making you want to puke, this kind of parental sputter can make you feel sort of dumb and childish. A few parents will want to lock their kids in the house until they are eighteen.

That they act this way is not really your parent's fault. They just never expected you to get serious about someone of the opposite sex until you were almost ready to be married. They don't know how to react!

phone trouble

People who like each other end up talking on the phone a lot—and I do mean *a lot*! This can be incredibly boring. I know plenty of kids who run out of things to say and end up just listening to the person breathe. One kid in our group actually fell asleep with the phone next to her ear while listening to her boyfriend sleep.

If you start spending a lot of time talking on the phone, expect your parents to flip out. They will undoubtedly give you a telephone time limit or make you pay for extra charges on your cellphone. Or they may cut off your tongue. This is fair since the house phone needs to be shared by everyone, and if you have a cellphone your parents are probably paying the bill. And your dad may not agree that a call from "Bubba" is as important as the call he is expecting from his boss.

> **Don't make your special friend feel obligated to call you.**

A word of advice might be helpful to those of you who find yourself wanting to spend hours talking to your boyfriend or girlfriend via the phone or internet: some people don't really like to talk on the phone or spend all day chatting on the internet. (If *you* are one of these people, make sure you tell your boyfriend or girlfriend right away.) Be careful not to make your special friend feel obligated to call you. Once people start to feel obligated and expected to do certain things, they often start feeling trapped and want out of the relationship.

A long time ago only desperate girls called boys. Although times have changed, there is still a bit of wisdom in letting boys do the telephone calling or online connecting. My reasoning is simple. If a boy thinks he is pursuing you, he will tend to stay interested. (Right, guys?) We seem to find what is out of our grasp very appealing. If a boy thinks he is being chased—well, he may use you for a little while, but he won't really like being chased for very long. In other words, a wise girl doesn't call a boy she likes—no matter how much she wants to—unless she is invited to.

broken hearts

If you are having a serious boyfriend/girlfriend relationship, I want you to think carefully about what I am going to tell you next:

Expect to get dumped.

It happens to almost everyone sooner or later, and to some of us a whole bunch of times. Getting dumped really hurts, especially if you still have feelings for the person

who dumped you. You will feel rejected, crushed, angry, and even stupid for liking the person who hurt you.

Although getting dumped can be terribly painful, the pain won't kill you. You'll live and probably even find yourself attracted to someone else in a short time. Most of your friends will try to comfort you by telling you what a moron your old girlfriend or boyfriend was and by reminding you that there are "other fish in the sea." But such pearls of wisdom aren't always enough to comfort broken hearts.

After a breakup, expect your relationship with that other person to be a little bit weird. In fact, it may very *very* weird. What I mean is that most people discover that going back to being "just friends" after a romantic relationship is next to impossible. This is especially true if you have become physically involved. Your former boyfriend or girlfriend will probably avoid you, stop hanging out with you or your group, and possibly say some pretty harsh things about you. As you may find out, there is a price you pay for a relationship.

sex

Even though most kids in Middle School don't have full-blown passionate romances, there are always a few who do. Sometimes older boys hound a girl, and sometimes kids from their own peer group wind up playing kissy-face. If you find yourself in that category, pay special attention to the rest of this c h a p t e r because we are going to talk about sex.

If you have questions that this book doesn't answer, please talk to an adult you can trust.

Kids in Middle School often have tons of questions about sex and dating. Most of them are too shy or embarrassed to ask those questions. Some go on to the Internet to see what they can learn—and get a quick scorching of ever-present porn, but few real answers. Although I don't want to make this book into a manual on sex, I would like to give you some tips that will help you keep this area of your life from smacking into trouble. If you have questions that I don't answer, please talk to an adult you can trust. She or he may get embarrassed too, but will probably try to answer your questions.

Sex begins whenever you get physical with another person. *Having sex* means the act of intercourse. *Sexuality* in a relationship starts when your body takes hold of someone else's. Some kids start to play with sex while still in Middle School—but like playing with fire, a few who are not careful end up getting burned.

Sex is a good thing. It is a gift from God. He created it, designed all the parts and pieces, and installed the engine that drives it. But He also put conditions on it for our own good and for the good of those around us. For example, imagine that you have been given a car that is a drag racer. There is a time and place to use a drag racer and a time and place *not* to use one. The proper place is on a drag strip; the improper place is on the streets downtown. Using your drag racer to get to the mall will endanger your life and the lives of others. Drag racers are made for a special purpose.

Sex is a bit like a drag racer. You can start its engine and sit behind the wheel, but once you back it onto the neighborhood street, you're asking for trouble. Sex is an act meant for marriage, just as the drag racer is meant for a drag strip.

Let me speak frankly: Despite what you see on TV or in the movies, despite the messages from magazines and songs, and regardless of what friends, parents or relatives may do or say—having sex before a lifelong commitment to another person (marriage) is wrong in God's eyes.

danger zones

You might want to keep a few things in mind if you end up playing around with sex. First of all, expect anything you do physically with your boyfriend (or even girlfriend) to be told around the school. This isn't very nice, but it's the way things are. Some boys like to brag about how far they got with their girlfriends. That kind of bragging is a creepy thing to do. Kids like to talk and spread rumors, which will be doubly true after you break up. You are giving others ammunition when you have sex with someone.

> **Having sex before a lifelong commitment to another person (marriage) is wrong in God's eyes.**

If you make out with lots of people, you'll get a bad reputation. If you are a girl, you may find boys trying to pick up on you. They'll want to mess around with you because they think that they can get you to play around sexually without too much effort. If you are a boy, girls will think you are insincere and have a one-track mind—a dirt track.

Sex is like going downhill on a bicycle. You get lots of sensation, you pick up speed and distance as you go, but putting on the brakes becomes harder and harder. And as you may know from experience, the faster you go on a bike, the nastier the results are if you crash. The same is true with sex. If you get yourself into a situation where you are having sex or even coming close to having it, you may find a big surprise waiting for you down the road.

Many kids who want to do the right thing have asked me, "How far should I go in playing around with sex?" The best advice I can give is to keep private things private. In other words, if you consider a part of your body private and personal, keep it that way and don't share it with others.

Don't buy dumb lines like: "If you love me, you'll let me," "What's the matter? Are you a prude?" and "Why not? Everyone else does." These are old tricks used by insincere people to get their way. The funny thing is, although these tricks are ancient, people still fall for them.

Make it easy on yourself—avoid sexual temptations. If you knew the neighbor's pit bull was hungry, would you hang over the fence eating a pastrami sandwich? Would you dress up like T-bone steak and dance around in front of the mutt? If the dog took part of your hand along with your sandwich, most people would say that you asked for it.

Make it easy on yourself—avoid sexual temptations.

one last word

Sexual desire is like a hungry dog. Keep temptation out of reach. For example, don't fill your head with garbage from the Internet, sex magazines, steamy movies or videos. This kind of stuff is easy to find and plenty of people, especially guys, look at it. But it won't help you keep your mind off sex.

If you have a boyfriend or girlfriend, avoid situations in which you can get physical without being discovered. Don't invite your boyfriend over while you are babysitting. Not only is this dumb, but you can also expect the little kids to squeal if they catch you. And don't have the person you adore come to

your house when you know you'll be alone. This kind of setting will make putting the brakes on sex very difficult to do.

Love and romance "Middle School style" can be fun and exciting if you are wise in the way you handle them—or it can be the start of a nightmare if not done the way God has designed. You make the choice!

surviving
middle school
chapter seven

I see naked people

*T*he young guys at the skatepark were laughing and giggling at the cellphone. I knew something weird was going on so I slowly wandered behind them to see what the commotion was about. Sure enough, one of the guys had downloaded a picture of a naked woman on his cellphone and was "sharing" his bit of art with his friends. His friends all seemed to want to become art collectors as well.

I bet this kid's mom had no idea what was coming up on the screen every time he flipped open his cellphone. And I bet she would have smacked him back to electronic prehistoric ages if she found out.

If you use a computer or cellphone, go to the movies or have a TV, you will see naked people—whether you are looking for them or not. Most of the time what is being hurled at your eyeballs is pornography; pictures designed to show sex or to get your brain to think about sex. (As if most Middle School kids need assistance to think about that subject!)

a serious subject

In the last chapter we talked about love and romance. Now I wanna bring up something that's related, but nowhere NEAR what real love and romance are. I want to be very honest with you about this subject and ask that you take what I tell you very seriously. *You are being preyed upon*—and you may not even know it. Somebody wants to put implants in your brain that will make handling modern technology in a way that is decent and honoring difficult—for the rest of your life.

Everyone knows that kids in Middle School—especially boys—have a natural curiosity and interest in sex. People also know that viewing pictures of naked people can become *very* addicting. Some rotten and perverted adults have decided that this is a good way for them to make a fortune in spite of what it does to their "customers." These people know that if you can get a young boy in the habit of going to naked lady sites or looking for places to get another jolt of electronic sex, you

may just create a steady customer for life.

Of course, they start you off with a bit of free "teaser" material to get you hooked; then as a boy grows along with his "habit" of chasing down pornography, sooner or later those who are laying the trap will be able to get money

out of the young man—he will PAY to see more and more of what they are offering.

Once you get yourself in the habit of viewing porn, breaking the addiction is *really* hard to do. Some little collection of sick brain cells in the back of your mind demand to see more, and more, and more! They cry and pout. They scream for their own way. Many people find that quieting those screaming cells is very difficult—giving into the begging of those twisted brain cells is far easier to do.

You've probably realized that those who sell flesh have flooded every possible area with their images. Even if you have no interest in seeing pornography, escaping it is hard as it pops up on e-mail messages or blinks on a website that by its name has nothing whatsoever to do with sex. (This is done intentionally by porn distributors buying website domains with innocent or even religious sounding names to use as a front for their material. This way they can fool those acting as watchmen for kids surfing online.)

Website blockers and safeguarding software can help, but the slimeballs often figure out a way around those efforts. Plus, for every Middle School kid who is trying to avoid pornography there are three others who are diving into it and, like the kids at the skate park, trying to share it with others. You'll find that some kids who use computers in your school have figured out ways to get around the defense systems and are pulling up porn when the teacher isn't watching.

You'll discover that, especially if you're a guy, keeping from getting pulled into this whirlpool of smut will take real effort on your part. You will have to click off the website, avert your eyes, change the channel or walk away. And if you avoid visual porn, songs with lyrics that are just as sick and twisted may assault you from a friend's iPod or stereo. You will need a lot of discipline and self-control not to indulge your curiosity and interest.

> **Keeping from getting pulled into this whirlpool of smut will take real effort.**

While God has created us so that the average guy finds the image of a woman with little or no clothes to be very, very attractive and interesting, His plan is for that crazy wild desire to be something special and private between two people with wedding rings on their fingers, not something to toss on a public website.

Don't kick yourself for being tempted to want to see naked people. It is normal and natural. Kick yourself for giving into the temptation.

Many guys who develop a porn viewing habit in Middle School will experience a lot of tears, flying vases and swinging rolling pins later in life. That's when when he finds that even though he is married, his habit remains and that the nasty little habit is discovered by his wife. Or perhaps worse, the shame he would feel if his children discover it. Some people have their brains and souls scarred for life by plunging into the world of cyber porn. You should avoid it like poison.

Do your best to keep the naked people from coming around.

If your parents haven't installed one yet, ask them to buy a program that blocks this kind of trash coming from cyberspace. If you are hanging out with a bunch of guys who are turning into perverts or sex fiends, you need to find some new friends. Do the best you can to keep the naked people from coming around. Trust me. They aren't trying to have a conversation with you when they pop up on your screen.

cyber fiends

The computer that gives you access to so much material, both good and bad, has also turned into one of the more popular ways to meet friends and talk with others. On the computer you can chat with your friends at the speed of your fingers clicking away on the keys or by voice and video hook ups.

For some people the cyber world is more than just getting information or talking to friends. It is a chance to enter the world as another person entirely, to make believe and never be discovered. Some people create their new identity and post themselves online as a creature that is completely different from the person actually writing. Sometimes these new identities are goofy and mostly harmless fun.

But sometimes they show a troubled darker side of a person's heart.

As you may be aware, there are all kinds of strange people cruising the Internet chat rooms to find curious or vulnerable kids. The young babe whose picture pops up on the chat-room may be a pot-bellied, greasy, sixty-year-old perverted man in pretend mode trying to lure kids into talking about sex—or in

some cases, meeting with him. Some of these freaks even talk kids into taking photos of themselves with little or no clothes on and sending those digital snapshots to them. Imagine where all those photos end up!

Yes, such activity is super sick. Yes, it is illegal. And yes, those pervs go to jail if they are caught. But every year thousands of kids are baited into these online cesspools created by adults who are pretending they are somebody else. Yuck!

The best rule of thumb is to NEVER chat with people whom you don't know in real life. If you go to a chat-room, go to one that has rules or is monitored. (For instance, one church set up a weekly chat-room for kids to come online and talk to their youth pastor about any questions they had about the Bible—it was pretty cool).

NEVER give away information while on the computer.

Also, NEVER give away information while on the computer. There is absolutely no reason why anyone you don't know needs your phone number, your address, your school or your photo.

While I am talking about technology and devices, I might as well mention a couple more...

cellphone do's and don'ts

By now you have probably noticed that every other kid has a cellphone. (When my kids bugged me for one I gave them a can with a string in it. They were not amused.) Cellphones are handy tools to stay in touch, take photos, play songs, do math, keep you company on a lonely night and light the way in the dark. In the near future most cellphones will have a GPS (Global Positioning Satellite) receiver in them so that parents can not only hear that you are okay, but they can also see if you *really* are at the mall or not.

But some people are slaves to their cellphones. They HAVE to answer the crummy things no matter where they are or what they are doing. They run out of the movies when their cellphone starts vibrating (or are thrown out if it starts ringing).

Some people have no sense about using cell phones politely. Believe it or not, one kid at our church had his cellphone ring during the sermon. Not only did he answer his phone, but he also actually was having a conversation while everyone else was listening—or trying to listen—to the pastor. Even worse, he was in the front row. And boy was he embarrassed when the pastor stopped his sermon and asked him not to do his personal phone business during church. Dumb kid!

Cellphones should be turned off when in church. Cellphones should be turned off when in class. Cellphones should be turned off when at movies or concerts. And cellphones should be turned off while at funerals. (And other places as well.)

If you break a conversation in order to answer a call from another friend, you are rude.

> **Cellphones should not pre-empt the people you are talking to face-to-face.**

Oh, and cellphones should not be used to store pictures your mother wouldn't want you to have, either!

dvd's, tv and movies

What would you do if you had eight years to spend on something? Say you spent eight years practicing guitar—chances are, you would be a pretty amazing performer. Or, if you spend eight years working on sharpening your skills with magic and slight of hand, I'd be calling you "Mr. Houdini." You could probably even make your annoying sister disappear!

But guess how average Americans will spend eight years of their lives: watching TV. How booooring! Yep, EIGHT YEARS out of the average life span is spent in front of the glowing screen. That's living life through the adventures of others.

There's gotta be a better way to live! Learn to turn the idiot box off and watch only the shows that you really want to watch. There are much better ways to spend your life and much better things to feed your brain.

Speaking of feeding your brain, you probably know that all movies have a rating system. The idea behind the rating system is to let people know what movies are full of terrible stuff and what movies are decent enough to see. Of course, this system doesn't work so well. Most of us have scratched our heads at how one movie without anything nasty or bad in it gets rated "R" and some really foul, rude and obscene movie makes it through with a PG 13 rating. You probably think I am going to go on some kind of rant about not watching R rated movies and how Hollywood is trying to make Christians look dumb. But that is not what I want to say.

All I want to say about TV, Movies, DVD's and the rest of the media you get your paws on can be summed up with a couple of pieces of advice:

> **Just because you start a movie doesn't mean you have to finish it.**

First, be wise. If a movie has nothing of real importance to offer, or if it is finding humor by dredging around the basement of human culture, maybe you should pass on watching it. And I think most people, even Middle Schoolers, have a pretty good idea of which HBO specials to avoid, which TV programs are poop with a laugh track, and what films are full of nudity, profanity and pointless hatred.

Second, just because you start a movie doesn't mean you have to finish it. There are no movie police around whose job it is to make you sit out a film that turned out to be nothing but projected garbage. I have walked out of several movies because my values and sensibilities were being offended.

I got my money back too.

video games

Lemme slide one thing in here for the guys. Video games are COOL! The graphics keep getting better and better, and the gameplay—especially when playing with others as a team—is nothing short of exhilarating. LAN parties are popular weekend events for many of my Middle School friends, and all the guys (and a few girls) know how to play WAY better than I do.

I've noticed, though, a tendency among some of the guys to create an alternative online gaming personae for themselves. They go online and become a swaggering, cussing, sneering person who in no way reflects the person that they REALLY are.

Remember, you are in control of your fingers. You don't have to cuss via your keyboard. You can let your gaming actions speak for themselves. And, you need to be mindful that the online world isn't "real"—it is what you make of it.

music devices

Music playing devices are getting smaller, cooler and more powerful. Some play videos and store lots of pictures. Before long they will invent one that gives you a back massage as well!

With all the music that is available and all the music that Middle School kids store on their iPods or have stored on their computer, you need to figure out what

WHATCHA LISTENING TO?

is worth listening to and what, while possibly musically pleasing, is full of verbal trash or worse.

While parents usually are concerned with the stuff their kids are putting in their brains, most of them have lost the ability to keep track of it all. They simply trust that their kids are making wise decisions in the music department. And judging by the four-letter foulness blasting through many earphones of Middle School kids, their trust is not well-founded.

I know that you can easily be convinced that you aren't affected by lyrics, even bad ones. And I know that not all music is raunchy. But what you feed your mind is what grows there. Feed it trash and you will start to think trash. Feed your brain good stuff and good stuff grows.

If you want a good rule of thumb, imagine that Jesus asks to listen to what you have on your iPod. If you would be embarrassed to have Him listen to your music, if you would start making lame excuses such as "ah, um, I only listen to the sound", then you need to do some editing of your music selections.

Better yet, do some exploring and be the one to discover new, cool music. There is a whole world of red-hot music that most of your friends have never heard, but would probably like if they were exposed to it. Young men and women who love music and who love God create much of that music. Sometimes it is called "Christian" music—but most of the performers would rather just say that they are Christians through whom God writes

His music. Sometimes the songs may talk about God; sometimes they may talk about something else. But whatever they talk about, the perspective is much healthier than those songs written by the sick puppies out there.

You may wonder where you can find the kind of music I am talking about. To give you a small taste, there is a free CD in the back of this book with a pile of music that you just might find really cool. There is also a cool website where you can find even more of this kind of music: *www.echoessms.com*.

Trust me. It is worth checking out! Your brain will thank you. Your heart, too. Maybe your friends as well for turning them on to a hot new band they have never heard before.

If Jesus borrowed your iPod, I bet He would be stoked.

And if Jesus were to borrow your iPod—well, I bet He would be stoked.

one last word

You know that by now these areas of life are pretty much out of your parents' ability to control. It now all comes down to you. What choices will you make when it comes to entertainment and using modern technology? Will you use it for good? Will you feed your heart, mind and soul with stuff that isn't just sewer contents in a different package?

What you decide says a lot about you—for good or bad, for wise or foolish. I hope that you don't join the "Idiot Circus." It already has enough clowns.

surviving middle school
chapter eight

how to avoid flunking

*M*any kids who did pretty well in elementary school end up with dismal grades their first year in Middle School. The main reason for the drop is that kids are getting used to a new system: multiple teachers with varying demands, an increased homework load, and lots and lots of distractions.

In this chapter I'd like to give you a few tips on how to keep your grades from sliding into the basement. Most of the stuff I'll tell you is pure common sense. If you get a grasp on them now, they will serve you the rest of your school life and possibly far beyond.

> **The struggle of learning is not so much a matter of skill as it is a matter of attitude.**

be positive

You'll notice every kind of attitude from students in every class. There'll be everything from kids who are only there physically to kids who just need a passing grade or they will be taken out back and shot by their parents. Attitudes are funny things: if you think that you will get rotten grades in school, then you probably will! And if you set your mind on getting good grades, you usually will get them, too. The struggle of learning is not so much a matter of skill as it is a matter of attitude. Skill in a subject can be learned, but attitudes come from within.

be prepared

Come to class every day with everything you need for the business at hand. For example, make sure you have your books, a notebook filled with paper, sharpened pencils with a good eraser (or extra lead for your mechanical pencils), a pen and whatever else is required for that class. Try to avoid being one of those

people who always need to ask to borrow pencils or paper from someone else.

be organized

Once you have your class supplies, you need to get organized. Just before school starts each year, almost every store carries those cool binders that have dividers for each class, a place to stash pencils, a built-in calculator, handy charts that will allow you to convert any measurement into metric, a place for pictures of your dog, the Constitution translated into fourteen languages, and an emergency life raft. With a tool like this, you can have an organized life with very little effort.

Most students *start* their school year organized. But after the second week or so, things will begin to deteriorate. By keeping your school stuff neat, you'll be able to find what you need when you need it. And being neat will keep you from losing or damaging important papers. Papers are more impressive if they aren't dog-eared or streaked with today's lunch. Neatness takes time, but in the end it saves lots of time—time that you otherwise have to spend looking for lost papers or assignments.

catch the system

In each of your classes, your teacher will have requirements that you will have to fill in order to get a decent grade. This way of doing things is called the *system* for that particular class. Some classes will be easy—all you have to do is show up with a pencil and you get a good grade! Other classes will be much tougher. You've already experienced systems to some degree in elementary school. Then you only had to get used to one or two teachers; now, you have to figure out about six.

In order to keep track of what is required for each class, pay close attention, especially for the first several weeks. Write in a notebook everything your teachers tell you to do. Some kids use special little notebooks to keep track of assignments. Others use binders or planners.

avoid goof-offs

If at all possible, avoid sitting around people who will keep you from getting your work done in class. If you have friends who try to talk to you or if you sit between two guys who carry on daily spit-wad wars, see if you can move to another seat. If you *really* want to position yourself to concentrate in class, sit right up front. That will keep you on your toes. The only drawback that *I* can think of to sitting up front is if your teacher doesn't say it, but sprays it.

suit up

To avoid doing poorly in P.E., follow one simple rule: suit up and play. Many schools require the students to change into gym clothes for PE, and few kids never suit up (or dress out). Some of them think they are too cool to play organized sports. Some are afraid of the ball or of sweat. Some consistently forget their gym clothes at home. Some are too timid to change their clothes in front of others. The typical coach does not take non-suits lightly. Your grades will be affected if you fail to suit up and play.

Sometimes a teacher will lower your P.E. grade if you forget to take your gym clothes home and wash them. If you are lucky, your school may have a washer and dryer spot where you can wash your stuff there.

do your homework

Even though having to attend school all day long and then getting stuck with more work on top of that seems very unfair, homework is a sad fact of life. Most teachers are very serious when they say that homework projects must be completed, so get used to them. I realize some elementary schools give out a little homework, but nothing like what you'll be assigned in Middle School.

Homework is a sad fact of life.

Since you're going to be stuck with homework, make the best of it. If you can develop a few good habits and a little discipline, you'll be able to get your homework done quickly and still maintain its quality. The following tips will help make homework as painless as possible:

- *Find the right place.* Don't try to do homework in a place where you're going to be bothered by your little sister eating your papers or your folks tripping over you. Find a desk or table that has good lighting and is far away from the rest of the family. And sit up! The kids who try to finish their homework as they lie on their beds usually fall asleep with their noses in their textbooks. Some people try to do their homework while watching TV, listening to music, or talking on the phone. That makes working difficult. The fewer interruptions and distractions you have, the faster you'll finish your work and be free to do what you really want to do with your afternoon or evening. In giving you this advice, I realize that what might distract one person is background noise to another. Use common sense as you decide what kinds of conditions you can really work under and what kinds will keep you from getting on with the job.

- *Avoid snacking.* This bit of wisdom comes from the common experience of having just completed a lengthy homework assignment and knocking a glass of milk all over it. Most teachers don't like to receive papers with gooey bits of pizza still stuck to them. Give yourself a break and eat in the kitchen. You'll be glad that you did!

- *Do it now.* This goes for finishing homework, studying for tests, and working on any other projects that must be done by a deadline. There is nothing worse than feeling panic swell

up inside as you realize that you have one night left to complete a science notebook that you should have been working on all month. Even though it's a drag, work on your projects *before* you hit that anxiety level. Save yourself the stress and probable failure by getting these kinds of jobs done before a course is over. This may mean practicing "delayed gratification" and refusing to do what you want to do right when you want to. But putting off pleasures for the moment will make you enjoy them even more when the work at hand is completed. And, do your weekend work on Friday night rather that on Sunday night—you'll find that the weekend is a whole lot more enjoyable because no assignments hang over your head.

- *Work in blocks.* Working under self-imposed pressure can increase the quality of your study time. Give yourself a certain time period within which to complete a task. Refuse to quit or take a snack break until that block of time is used up or the job is finished, whichever comes first.

- *Develop work integrity.* Sometimes you will be tempted to let a friend, older brother or sister, or even one of your parents do your homework for you—or at least give you all the answers. This may get your work done quickly, but will hurt you in the long run. This principle is especially true for swiping essays straight from the web.

- *Make no excuses.* I'm amazed at how often people with unfinished homework assignments blame some disaster. I can assure you that your teacher has already heard all the sad-eyed stories about homework-eating dogs, paper-snatching tornadoes, and notebook-snatching thieves. Don't even bother telling those stories. You'll just make yourself look stupid.

cheaters never win

Once you get the homework habit down, there's one more little thing you need to think about: cheating. Some people spend more energy figuring out clever ways to cheat on class exams than they would have spent studying for them. You've probably seen many of their sneaky devices: cheat sheets written on thin paper and shoved up sleeves, answers written on hands or forearms in ink, or (my favorite) carefully created answer sheets placed in the chambers of clear pens.

Most teachers have seen all of these tricks—many times. If you are busted for cheating, not only will your grade suffer, but also you will heap shame on yourself. And if you are a Christian you'll do damage to the reality of your faith.

You see, cheating is stealing and deception. If you get your answers from someone else's paper, you are stealing that work. If you get your answers from a cheat sheet, you are lying to your teacher about what you know.

You'd think that kids who claim to be Christians would know that cheating is wrong and would never do so. But you and I know that the temptation to cheat is so strong that some kids give into it over and over again.

difficult classes

If you are really trying to do your best in a class and still get poor grades, you may be in a class that is too advanced for you. Perhaps you have not yet mastered the foundational material that you must know in order to make it in the class.

One seventh-grade student I knew was only an average math student, but was somehow placed in the most advanced math class his school offered. Try as he could, the best grade he could manage was a D. The school kept him in the class for the entire year. In the meantime, he fell further and further behind, lost in a cloud of confusion and frustration. Somebody in the scheduling office had goofed.

The next year he transferred down a notch to a class almost as advanced as his last one but still far beyond his limits. But by this point, he had given up on math and had developed a strong distaste for the subject.

If you think this kind of situation is happening to you, go straight to your counselor and ask to be transferred to an easier class. And don't be ashamed to do so. A simple schedule change can make a big difference.

one last word

Although getting good grades comes easier to some than others, most of us can get pretty good grades with a combination of common sense and a bit of personal discipline. The effort is good practice for the adult world. Kids who always look for the easy way out often play now and pay later. I hope they enjoy working in car washes for the rest of their lives.

surviving
middle school
chapter nine

dealing with the authorities

*H*ave you ever watched an old Western movie? One of the standard gimmicks in those films is to help you know who the good guys and bad guys are by the hats they wear. The good guys wear white hats and have shiny white teeth; the bad guys wear black hats, need a good shave and have black goo covering their pearlies.

Come to think of it, you can figure out almost everybody's role in those movies by looking at his or her hat: old ladies wear funny bonnets, stuffy town-folk wear derby hats, the undertaker wears a crumbled top hat, and the beautiful damsel wears no hat at all. Before the actors in these old films even speak a line or sing a love song to a cow on the prairie, you understand their roles in the drama by the hat they wear.

As you go through life in Middle School, you'll meet a lot of people who are wearing different hats. They are the "authorities" in charge of you. Each one has a role to play in the day-to-day drama of Middle School—and you may be surprised to discover that some of these people intentionally put on black hats.

Let's check out the various authorities you will bump up against as you travel through Middle School and then consider some tips that can keep that trip from becoming unpleasant.

I am sure you assume that every adult in your school is an authority. This may be true, but there are various levels of authority. The school janitor is an authority, but has nowhere near the power of a vice principal. So who are your school authorities and what do they do?

the principal

The principal, the boss of the school, wears a white hat. The principal wants to make you happy, your parents happy, the teachers happy, and their bosses at school district central happy. Most school principals don't get involved in the everyday life of the average student. They present the blue ribbons, give the speeches, handle big, big problems, and do lots of paperwork. You will probably see the principal around, but rarely will you be called into his or her office—except by mistake. If you go to a small school, you'll be more likely to see and talk to the principal. If you go to a large school, you may see the principal only on special occasions.

the vice principal

The vice principal usually wears a black hat. In big schools there may be several vice principals. If you get called into the vice principal's office, start sweating bullets, because the V.P. handles the really nasty jobs at school. Vice Principals deal with the guys who blow up toilets or get into fights. They handle the troublemakers, chronic truants, and those caught selling school secrets  to terrorists. They have the power to kick you out of school, make you do grounds cleanup—or worst of all—call your parents. Mind your manners when the V.P. comes around.

Some V.P.'s are actually very nice people who have taken on a job that is guaranteed to make them unpopular with a slice of kids on campus. Other V.P.'s take the job because they can't find steady work as professional torturers anywhere else.

school secretaries

Many schools have a battalion of people who maintain attendance records, handle paperwork, and keep you from see-

ing your counselor if you are without an appointment. Most of them have seen every trick in the book. They can tell when you have tried to fake one of your parent's signatures on an excuse note. Probably they are the true brains behind your school. They wear brown hats—they aren't good guys or bad guys. They're like the townspeople in the western movies—always there, but you're not sure why.

counselors

Most schools assign you to an adult to be your guiding angel through Middle School. This person is your counselor. If you do a lousy job of keeping your grades up, chances are you will end up in the counselor's office.

Counselors wear white hats. In the ten minutes that they have you in their office, they want to become your pal. They are probably the ones who will contact your parents if you are bombing in your classes. They also handle minor discipline problems for the vice principals. If you are caught chewing gum in class for the third time, you may find yourself sitting in the counselor's office for the rest of the class period rather than being stretched out on the torture rack in the V.P.'s office.

campus security

On some Middle School campuses, you will discover one or two people wearing what look like police uniforms, complete with walkie-talkies and badges. At first glance you may wonder whether you have enrolled in school or are serving a prison sentence.

They are the security guards, also known as "rent-a-cops." Their job is to make sure undesirables from the community don't come around to hassle smaller kids like you and to keep loonies and drug dealers away. Unless you do something terrible (like littering) you will probably never be bothered by these folks. But be careful, they wear black hats.

teachers

Teachers are the main authority figure you will encounter on a regular basis. They each have their own style of discipline and control. Some will bust you for the slightest infraction of the rules while others walk around in a daze as the kids run amuck. Most teachers wear white hats.

Try to not get on a teacher's bad side right off the bat—doing so will haunt you for the rest of the year. Just as you will develop an impression of each teacher during the first week

of school, each teacher will also have a first impression of you. If you act up, fall asleep at your desk, come in late, or mouth off on the first day, your teacher will probably consider you in a less-than-positive light.

Even though teachers are supposed to deal with you in a neutral fashion, they are human and cannot help giving breaks to those they like—and drilling to the wall those they don't. Like most authorities, teachers like to be right or superior in their judgments and do not take it very well if students put them in their place. I know about this fact from hard experience.

Teachers are human.

I once had a devout Mormon for an English teacher. During the course of a lecture, she made the comment: "The Bible teaches that black people are inferior." As a Christian, I knew that this statement was absolute nonsense. I also knew that for over a hundred years Mormons believed that no black person could reach what they called the *priesthood* in their religion. (By the way, the Mormon Church has since abandoned this teaching.)

My hand shot up. "Excuse me, teacher, but could you tell me where the Bible says that blacks are inferior?" The class hushed. Who was this brave soul challenging the deep and unending well of knowledge residing in this teacher?

She responded with irritation, "Well, I could, but I don't have a Bible." The class shifted its view back to me. Had I been checked? Was this the end of the Defiant One? Never!

Ever resourceful, I produced a Bible from under my chair and offered it to her. She thumbed through the pages for a few minutes, reddened in the face, and mumbled, "I can't seem to find it right now, but I'm sure it's in there."

Being a dumb kid and sensing blood, I continued after my prey by giving a little speech that would be my undoing (academically) in the class. "Well, I really doubt that what you claim is in the Bible can actually be found there. I suggest that you not make claims about things this serious unless you can back then up with proof."

By now I knew the whole room was cheering (silently, of course). I was David and she was Goliath! The mouse that roared! The small, insignificant insect of a student single-handedly toppling the mighty authority of the classroom! Hooray!

I left the class feeling that I had scored big time, and only when grades came out did I realize that I was earning a return on my investment. I suffered with D's in the class for a semester. Finally, after asking for and receiving a transfer to another English class, I ended the year with B's.

> **You will find that your teachers are fair, caring, and eager to be accurate in what they teach.**

The moral? Buck authority if you must, but be willing to pay the consequences. For the most part, though, you will find that your teachers are fair, caring, and eager to be accurate in what they teach.

coaches

Although coaches *are* teachers, they are different from the other kinds of teachers you will meet. Generally, lipping off to coaches is unwise since they may use you as a rag to wipe off home plate. Even worse, they may tell you to "run laps", which is fine if you are a gazelle, but a drag if you are an eleven-year-old kid. Coaches are also the lucky teachers who get to wear shorts and T-shirts all day long as part of their jobs. They usually wear white hats.

subs

You have had substitute teachers before. These poor souls come willingly into a class that is without their regular teacher and try to keep the animals occupied.

Of course, as soon as kids in the class hear that they are having a sub, they start making plans to switch seats and identities. Kids who try to pull these pranks naturally think that they are really creative and funny and that their sub is so dumb that he or she will never catch on. Actually, subs know all about this trick and *assume* that you are not who you claim to be.

If subs wore hats, they would probably wear party hats since most of the time they have you watch videos rather than do work.

parents: the final authority

Of all the authorities in your Middle School life, your parents are still the ones with major influence. Their hats are whiter-than-white.

Sometimes parents have a hard time when their kids go into Middle School. They feel that they are losing the ability to direct and control the events in their kids' lives as they once did.

To add to this confusion, many Middle School kids seek more and more independence from their parents. They want to be individuals and make their own decisions, decisions that may sometimes go against their parents' wishes.

As time goes on, you may find yourself getting into domestic squabbles with your parents. The rocky spots might arise from just about anything: clothes, hairstyles, makeup, time spent on the phone or computer, chores, grades, friends—you name it.

If you know what actions and attitudes that parents are looking for, you have an advantage with this "prime authority" in your life. Most parents are very reasonable and will grant you more and more liberty if your show them you are in control. Here are some attitudes and actions that parents want to see before they will lengthen your leash.

Here are some attitudes and actions that parents want to see...

Act responsibly.

Parents need to see that you are not a flaky kid. This means that you need to do your chores without being told and clean up the messes you make without waiting for the "maid" to do it.

Do a good job on your chores or projects instead of trying to get by with the least amount of effort. For example, if your job is to sweep the garage or driveway, move stuff and don't just sweep around it. Get in the corners and pick up the debris with a dustpan instead of blasting it into the neighbor's yard.

Responsibility means carrying your weight and not being

a burden on someone else. It means being on time, or at the very least having the courtesy to call if there is some reason you will be late. And responsibility is showing wisdom by avoiding bad situations or doing stupid things like shooting the pesky neighbor kid with your Airsoft gun.

Communicate.

Parents want to know what you are thinking and feeling. They need you to give them more than one-syllable responses to their questions. They really do need you to ask their advice from time to time instead of just asking for money.

Like everyone else, parents need to be told that they are loved. Be sure to tell them often. Don't think that telling them you love them shows weakness or is a corny thing to do.

Make your parents proud of you.

Would your folks be proud of you if they knew everything that you're doing? Make that your goal. If you find yourself hiding your activities consistently and hoping your parents won't find out, you are probably into some pretty sad stuff. And you know that God may not be too happy with how you are conducting your life, either.

Obey.

Obedience isn't always easy, but you need to listen to your parents and obey them even when you don't want to. When a kid starts to rebel, many parents just tighten the screws. When a kid obeys, they let up. It's that easy.

Some kids complain that if they did everything their parents asked them to do, they would end up with no life at all. That is rarely the case. Most parents simply need to see that you still know who's the boss.

Show gratitude.

A major gripe of most parents is that kids are ungrateful little creeps. From my perspective as a longtime youthworker, I have to say that this is a valid complaint. Kids rarely take the little bit of effort required to tell their parents how much they appreciate what has been done for them. Just a few kind words make all the difference in the world.

Suppose some friend wants you to feed her every time she comes to your house. If she never said, "Thank you" when you rounded up a plate of goodies for her, but instead just dug right in, how would you feel? Or suppose a friend wants you  to lend him money or buy him stuff when you go to the mall because he keeps forgetting his money at home? Imagine that the whole time this was going on, the most thanks you ever got was something mumbled under his or her breath. Before long you will feel used big time by this so-called friend. You never hear an expression of gratitude, merely of expectation.

Parents don't like feeling used, either. They give, not because it's expected, but because they love. You'll be miles ahead if you show them you are thankful!

one last word

Try out some of these tips. See if they help improve your life with the authorities you can't transfer from!

surviving middle school
chapter ten

how to avoid being a jerk

No normal person wants to be thought of as a jerk. To avoid being one isn't hard; you just have to avoid jerkish behavior! This chapter holds some hints about what you should do and what you should avoid doing to keep from becoming a genuine jerk. Pay close attention—once you earn the title of complete jerk, you'll have a hard time getting rid of it.

don't brag

The fastest way to make people dislike you is to try too hard to be liked and to brag about yourself. Sharing real experiences or events in the context of appropriate conversation is okay. For example, if some kids are talking about scary things they have done, you can say, "Yeah, the time I tried sky-diving was the scariest for me!" That is not bragging, nor is it busting into someone else's conversation with information about your skydiving accomplishment. Bragging is exaggeration ("...and then when both of my parachutes failed, I..."). When you brag, you try to make yourself seem  more important than everyone else ("It took more guts than all of you've got put together to jump out of that plane").

Most people are smart enough to know when to be impressed and when a story is being inflated with events that never really happened. (So make sure you *really* did jump out of a plane before spouting off about it.)Kids who think they are being fed a load of manure by some braggart will likely challenge him or her to the test. "So, you can break bricks with your forehead, huh? Well, here's a pile of bricks. Let's see ya do it!" This means instant jerkdom for the poor slob whose imagination got the best of him or her during a story telling session. *Don't brag!*

don't pose

Don't put on an act or try to be someone you are not. Posers are spotted in a minute. The skinny little kids smoking over in the corner or playing the role of a strutting gangster may think they look mature and cool, but they fail to realize that almost everyone is laughing at them for trying to be someone other than who they are. You are not Mr. Macho, a pro ball player, a movie star or fashion model; so don't try to act like one. Be who you really are.

don't blab

You may have some experience with this truth already. In fact, your parents probably dropped this lesson on you by saying, "If you can't say something nice, don't say anything at all." This shows that parents actually *are* right sometimes! Keep your mouth closed until you clear the content of your words with your brain.

Your mouth will get you into plenty of trouble.

If you are in trouble with the school bully, it may be because of something you said. If you make your best friend cry or hate you, no doubt it's because you said something thoughtless to her or about her. If you find yourself sitting on the toilet seat with a bar of Ivory soap bubbling in your mouth, perhaps you said that word without checking it through the proper filter and your dad happened to be around the corner at the same time. If you find yourself on your way to the office with a referral in your hand, you probably have opened your big mouth in class when wisdom said to keep quiet and study.

Yep! Your mouth will get you into plenty of trouble, so weigh what you are going to say before you crank up your lips and start them flapping.

This last word of advice is mainly for girls since they are the ones who consistently pass notes or write long letters or e-mails to each other. The stuff you send around class via person-to-person postal service is going to get read. The e-mails are going to get forwarded. This is fine if you don't have anything private in your notes. But if you record your personal feelings in your "Secret—Do Not Let Anyone Else See This Upon Threat Of Death" correspondence, they will be public knowledge by the end of the day. Don't write anything that will make you feel dumb about if others read it. A home diary with a lock and key is where private thoughts should be kept.

don't lie

When a liar tells you something, do you believe it? Probably not. The problem with being or becoming a liar is that after a while people will not believe anything you say. Your word will become as valuable as play money. A friend once told me, "Your word is the most valuable thing you have." People who cannot be trusted to tell the truth might as well be mute.

We feel miserable when we sense that we are not trusted. We are hurt when the people we want to impress think that we are a snake because what we say is not true. But such is a position we place ourselves in by our actions.

Liars are thought of as jerks. They have few friends. Even the members of their own families don't trust them. They usually don't even like themselves very well.

Do tell the truth—no matter how painful, ugly and condemning it is. Facing the bitter consequences of truthfulness is always better than lying.

don't use people

If you win the lottery—I mean the big, *big* one—and everyone in school finds out about it, do you think that you will be treated differently? You bet! Boys and girls will want to borrow money with no intention of paying you back; friends will show up that you never knew existed. You will be a very popular person. But not because of you—because of your bucks!

Nobody likes to be used. We would hate to have some cute guy get to know us just so he could meet one of our friends. We would not like having our friends hang around with us just so they could swim in our pool, jump on our trampoline or skate on our ramp. Yet, it's so easy to use friends.

People who are users or takers eventually find themselves friendless. Their former friends now call them jerks.

don't mooch

Don't get in the habit of borrowing money or things from other people. If you *do* have to borrow something—which happens from time to time—return it or pay it back promptly.

The sad thing about most moochers is that they don't realize they are mooching. Even though they have a closet full of clothes or a pile of DVD's that

they borrowed from friends and have never returned, they think that because they *intend* to give the stuff back, they don't have a problem. Wrong! Your goal should be to borrow as little as possible and return promptly what you have borrowed.

don't victimize

In the jungle, the fit survive and the weak perish. In school some people act the same way. They find smaller, younger, frailer targets and then have fun at their expense. Since you are just coming into a new school situation, you probably can sense what life would be like if all the bigger kids decided to pick on you. You would be miserable!

Often people decide to pick on kids who look different, are too fat, have crooked noses, different skin colors, or accents. Usually those kids cannot defend themselves and simply have to take the humiliation. Kids who tease in this way are first-class jerks—not to mention cowards.

> **Don't kick down a weaker person with your words or actions.**

You will find that kids in Middle School have an incredible capacity for cruelty. Some sickos will torture animals; others delight in pestering classmates. The thing that all of these losers have in common is that they pick on those weaker than themselves in order to get a laugh.

On occasion a group of kids will act like piranhas and go after an individual until he or she breaks into tears or fights back. Don't kick down a weaker person with your words or actions. The Bible warns that you will reap what you sow!

don't be flaky

Flakes are people you can't count on. They are unreliable, irresponsible, and careless. If your teacher assigns you to work in teams to create models of Egyptian pyramids, the flake of the group will never show up to work on the project outside of the classroom. And when they *are* in the classroom, they won't contribute much to the project. But when grades are handed out, they will want to get A's for the project everyone else completed. This makes for very hard feelings toward the flakes involved.

One friend of mine had the misfortune of being assigned to a project with *three* flakes. Because none of them showed up to help her with the project, she ended up doing the all the work by herself. When she turned in the "group" project, she attached a note explaining that the other girls hadn't helped with the assignment and that it had been a solo effort.

My friend received an A in the class and the three flakes flunked. Boy, were they angry! (One thing you will notice about true jerks is that they get angry with others for consequences that are their own fault.)

Flakes are people who refuse to take responsibility for their own actions or lack of actions. They make excuses—"The dog ate my homework assignment"; "We ran out of Pampers and I had to use all my extra notebook paper to diaper my baby sister"; "There was an eclipse of the sun and I thought it was the end of the world, so I said to myself, 'No sense in doing my homework!'" Or they say dumb things like, "I forgot," "I couldn't find it," or "I didn't hear the instructions." Flakes *never* say, "I was lazy and irresponsible." No—they blame their failures on the actions of someone or something else. This makes them jerks as well as flakes.

don't be a know-it-all

Sometimes you will come across kids who *have* to be right, even if they are completely wrong. They are stubborn, mule-headed, and unteachable. Being wrong is not bad, but trying to convince everyone that you are right, when clearly you're not, is stupid. It's okay to lose an argument. Changing your mind is not only permissible, but is sometimes also a good idea. You don't know and never will know everything. You don't have to. People will respect you for the things you do know. And they will respect you even more when you admit you've made a mistake or don't know something.

Even though everyone has an opinion, not everyone deserves to have one. I know very little about cars. I can drive them, fill them with gas, and change a tire—but other than that, I am a complete idiot. During a discussion with some friends who happened to be good mechanics, opinions were exchanged about which brands of cars are good machines. When asked my thoughts on the subject, I honestly couldn't answer; I had to disqualify myself. Oh, I had an opinion I could have offered, but it would have been based on my ignorance of how cars work. So I didn't say anything.

> **"Better to be quiet and be thought a fool than to open your mouth and remove all doubt."**

Keep your mouth shut if you are not really informed about a subject. An old saying goes, "Better to be quiet and be thought a fool than to open your mouth and remove all doubt."

don't cheat

I know that I've stressed this before, but none of us likes a cheater. We automatically think of people as jerks if they have to cheat to win. But as you know, cheating is a widespread habit and by the time you finish Middle School, you will have seen lots of it.

Sometimes a kid who would never think of cheating in sports cheats like crazy in academic classes. A cheater is a cheater. Cheaters will do anything, even if it is wrong, for personal gain. A person who develops this trait becomes a loser for life.

one last word

Being a jerk is preventable. A bit of thoughtfulness and care, some self-control, and concern for the other person will keep you from ever wearing the title, "Jerk."

Extra bonus material is included for you on the next three pages!

the F-Bomb

A lot of kids seem to think that Middle School is the time to *really* start swearing. Maybe because they see films where adults swear a lot, or maybe they hear older folks swear—I dunno, but there seems to be a marked increase in the desire to use those few four letter words.

Especially the "F-bomb."

You need to be aware that using cuss words doesn't make a person sound smart. In fact, doing so makes them sound stupid. If you need to rant and rave about something, there are far more creative words you can say than going back to the same tired old list of cuss words.

The amazing thing is how some people grab on to a foul word and use it all the time—as a verb, noun, adjective, pronoun etc. I want you to see how stupid this really is.

Let's imagine that the word "surf" is used to replace the F-bomb (which is a crude word for describing a good thing that God made: in this case, sexual activity.) I picked "surf" because I love to surf and it is a fun activity. What would happen if you used "surf" in your speech patterns instead of the F-bomb?

"What the surf are you doing here?"
"Surf off, Mother surfer!"
"What the surf is this?"
"Surf you!"

Sounds silly, right? Well, when you stop and think about it, using the F-bomb is just as dumb. In fact it's even dumber.

So—if you *need* to spout off, try a nice little substitute word, one that actually fits and is appropriate. If you don't sound a lot smarter, at least everyone will get a good laugh!

insults

Okay, making insulting jokes with your friends is fun, and sometimes you need just the right comeback for the moron who is trying to pick on you. So, here is a whole pile of hilarious comments, replies and asides.

But here's the deal: these insults are kind of like a drawer of knives. You need to use them wisely and appropriately. They are designed for fun, not for revenge. If you can't figure out how to use a hilarious insult, keep the knives in the drawer.

Here are the ground rules: Never use an insult to be mean. Never pick on someone who can't help what they are. For example, kids who are overweight, mentally challenged, or born with a distorted face are on the forbidden list when it comes to joking around. Picking on those people by laughing at them is not joking; it's cruel and stupid on the part of those who engage in it. Also, no ganging up—that's not fair. And finally, be smart enough to know who can take a joke or an insult and who can't.

So, here you go! Here's list of comebacks and responses that will show how clever and funny you really are—even though you had to steal them from this book.

- Anyone who told you to be yourself couldn't have given you worse advice.
- He's as smart as a bag of hammers.
- Are you always so stupid or is today a special occasion?
- As an outsider, what do you think of the human race?
- He's a smart as a box of hair.
- You're as useless as rubber lips on a woodpecker.
- You're as welcome as a rattlesnake at a square dance.
- Calling you stupid would be an insult to stupid people.
- Your dog is so stupid that he chases parked cars.
- You're so lousy that if you threw a rock at the ground, you'd miss.
- You're so stupid that you'd trip over the cord of a cellphone.
- You're so ugly that when you went to a haunted house they offered you a job.
- You're so ugly that you make blind kids cry.
- He has the attention span of a lightning bolt.
- He loves nature in spite of what it did to him.
- His mother should have thrown him away and kept the stork.
- He's so dumb that he sits on the TV and watches the sofa.
- The oven's on, but nothing's cooking.
- He's a few clowns short of a circus.
- She's a few fries short of a Happy Meal.
- She's a few Cokes short of a six-pack.
- He's a few peas short of a casserole.
- She's one taco short of a combo plate.
- She's a few feathers short of a whole duck.
- He has an intellect rivaled only by garden tools.
- She's as smart as bait.
- He doesn't have all his dogs on one leash.

more insults

- Her sewing machine's out of thread.
- His belt doesn't go through all the loops.
- She sets low personal standards and then consistently fails to achieve them.
- He's got a full six-pack, but lacks the plastic thingy to hold it all together.
- He's as bright as Alaska in December.
- One-celled organisms outscore him in IQ tests.
- The gates are down, the lights are flashing, but the train isn't coming.
- He's a couple of knights short of a Crusade.
- He's a few feet short of the runway.
- He's a few puppies short of a pet shop.
- His antenna doesn't pick up all the channels.
- She's eating with only one chopstick.
- He left the store without all of his groceries.
- She's one song short of a musical.
- Did your parents ever ask you to run away from home?
- Did your parents have any children that lived?
- Do you ever wonder what life would be like if you'd had enough oxygen at birth?
- He doesn't know the meaning of the word "fear"—but then again he doesn't know the meaning of most words.
- Don't let your mind wander—it's too little to be let out alone.
- Every person has the right to be ugly, but you abused the privilege.
- He has the IQ of lint.
- Have you considered suing your brains for nonsupport?
- Have you conversed with any plankton lately?
- He can open his mail with that nose.
- He can think without moving his lips.
- He comes from a long line of real estate people—they're a vacant lot.
- He does the work of three men: Moe, Larry, and Curly.
- He has one brain cell, and it is fighting for dominance.
- He is always lost in thought—it's unfamiliar territory.
- He is depriving a village somewhere of an idiot.
- His brain waves fall a little short of the beach.
- People would follow him anywhere, but only out of curiosity.
- I don't know what makes you so stupid, but it really works.
- I heard that your brother was an only child.
- I like you. People say that I have no taste, but I like you.
- I thought of you all day today. I was at the zoo.
- If brains were rain, you'd be a desert.
- If I ever need a brain transplant, I'd choose yours because I'd want a brain that had never been used.
- If idiots could fly, this would be an airport.
- If manure were music, you'd be an orchestra.
- If you give him a penny for his thoughts, you get change back.
- If you were a body of water, you'd be a kiddy pool.
- Ignorance can be cured. Stupid is forever.
- I'll never forget the first time we met—although I'll keep trying.
- I'm blonde, what's your excuse?
- I'm glad to see you're not letting your education get in the way of your ignorance.
- I'm going to memorize your name and throw my head away.
- I'm not as dumb as you look.
- I've seen people like you, but I had to pay admission.
- Let's play horse. I'll be the front end and you be yourself.
- Make a mental note—oh wait, I see you're out of paper.
- Now go away or I shall taunt you a second time.
- Perhaps your whole purpose in life is simply to serve as a warning to others.
- She's like Taco Bell. When people see her, they run for the border.
- So, a thought crossed your mind? Must have been a long and lonely journey.
- Some drink from the fountain of knowledge, but he just gargled.
- Some folks are so dumb that they have to be watered twice a week.
- They shot him through the stupid forest, and he didn't miss a tree.
- Whatever anyone says to you goes in one ear and out the other because nothing is blocking traffic.
- Whatever is eating you—must be suffering horribly.
- Never enter a battle of wits unarmed.

surviving middle school
chapter eleven

you need friends

I met Tom in the seventh grade. We hung out in the same spot before school and our friendship grew out of that casual acquaintance.

Tom was never a dynamic personality at school—although he did receive temporary fame when he cut off half of his index finger with a table saw. For a week his misadventure was the talk of the lunch table. When he came back to school, the kids gathered around him to get their first glimpse of the bloody stump. Later he used the handicap to good advantage by inserting the stump into this nostril and pretending to pick all the way to his brain. Yep, Tom's a talented guy.

We continued to hang out through high school and during the summer of our college years even though we went to schools in two different countries. Later we found ourselves working together in the same town and at the same company, and finally even moved to the same island in the Pacific—where we both ended up serving on the staff at the same church.

Tom and I have had a friendship that is the kind you usually think of when you think of friends—a friendship that lasts forever, in which you live next door to each other, mooch sugar from each other, goof off together, and laugh about old times. But in real life, our relationship is a pretty rare situation. Most of your friends will come and go; most of your friendships will end when you graduate (or sooner), and you'll begin developing a whole new batch of friends.

In the next few pages, let's talk about developing two kinds of friendships. One kind you may experience during your time in Middle School and, if you're fortunate, beyond.

The other kind is even more important and, believe it or not, will last forever.

Everyone needs friends. Even loners who say they would rather be alone need friends. The need for friends is a desire built into us by God. But not everyone knows how to make friends or, even more important, how to keep the friends they make.

be friendly

If you rarely talk and head straight for the corner when you're in a room full of people, or are so quiet that even your parents think that you're mute, then making friends may be difficult for you. To make friends you must extend yourself— say "Hi" and talk about subjects that are of common interest. The friendlier you are, the more friends you will make.

be loyal

A good friend doesn't act like a hummingbird, drinking nectar from your flower and then flying off when a more attractive flower appears. True friends don't run off or change sides when other kids appear.

Being loyal does not mean that you become blind. A true friend will step in front of another who is heading into hurtful behavior. A real friend cares.

be genuine

True friends are never two-faced. They do not pretend to be good and trusted friends in order to hear all your deep dark secrets and then blab them all around. If you are told something in confidence, keep it in confidence. I can only think of one exception: if a friend tells you about something that will harm her or him, like thoughts of suicide or that she or he uses drugs or is involved in a sexual relationship. Pass on those conversations to a responsible adult, but don't spread those confidences around school.

be well-rounded

Sometime two friends get so tight with each other that they leave everyone else out. They are together constantly; they spend the night at each other's homes, wear each other's clothes, develop secret-coded languages, and are so close you would swear they have become Siamese twins. We sometimes call them Klingons, (which sounds like "Cling-Ons." Get it?)

This is not always healthy for a friendship. The reason? Sooner or later you will burn the relationship out. It's kind of like this: remember the time you went on a food binge? Perhaps you were craving Fudgsicles. You ate those frozen delights by the box. People thought you were born with a wooden stick in your mouth. Then suddenly you changed. You overdosed on Fudgsicles. You no longer wanted them. They became unappealing, and you began to crave some other goodie.

This happens with people, too. If you want your friendships to last, don't make them so binding that you leave no room for anyone else!

be able to apologize

Even in a friendship, problems can develop. Misunderstandings come up or one of you does something stupid. These become turning points in the friendship: the friendship can continue or bust apart. What happens to the friendship depends on the willingness of one or both friends to admit mistakes and apologize. Saying, "I'm sorry" costs nothing, except for a bit of pride.

be kind

Cut-downs can be fun. Friends often joke around and put each other down in fun, but rarely with any seriousness. Yet sometimes put-down sessions turn bloody. Jokes are still jokes, but nobody laughs. The jabs that used to be arrows with rubber suction cups on the end are now barbed steel—intentional and well aimed.

Because of this, people will often tell you that it's wrong to play with cut-downs at all. I'm not going to tell you that, but it is important to learn when to stop teasing and what kind of put-downs should be avoided.

The most hurtful cuts are those that poke fun at what we can't change. Talking like Porky Pig to a kid who stutters is not funny; it's *mean*. Trying to hurt or destroy somebody with our put-down is not funny. It's cruel and is a sign that we are not true friends.

be honest

The Bible contains an interesting quote: "The slap of a friend can be trusted to help you, but the kisses of an enemy are nothing but lies." (Proverbs 27:6) True friends have to say things sometimes that are unpleasant in order to help us out. If you make a total fool out of yourself at the lunch table, a real friend will tell you. The truth may hurt, but at least it's the truth. If your fly is down, a true friend will let you know—in a quiet, kind way. (Not, "Hey! Look! His zipper's down!")

The truth may hurt, but at least it's the truth.

forever friends

No matter how many great friends you have or how popular you become, sooner or later you will need a friendship that is stronger than any human can offer you. You will need the friendship of the One who created you.

God is very interested in being your friend. But be warned: dealing with God is not like messing around with school friends. He is very powerful and insists that people keep their bargains. And He has to be approached with a great deal of respect.

C.S. Lewis, the great Christian writer, created a series of children's stories called the *Chronicles of Narnia*. (I am sure you have seen the movie.) In those stories Jesus is portrayed as a powerful lion. I have always thought that was a very good image of God. Imagine that an intelligent but ferocious lion wanted to be friends with you. You wouldn't treat him as you do your pet cat. You would approach him carefully and not tease him by pulling his whiskers. God wants to be your friend, but not in a casual, flippant manner. Remember, He is King and Creator of the universe.

As you have learned from your human relationships, real friendships are two-sided. If a person wants to be friends with another person who would prefer *not* to be friends, someone will get hurt. God wants to be your friend, but He will not force His friendship on you. You must want the friendship too.

But *saying* you want God to be your friend and *meaning* it are two different things. A desire to be God's friend must be demonstrated.

God has already gone a long way to prove that He wants to be your friend. Jesus once taught His disciples the greatest test of friendship that can be demonstrated. He said, "The greatest love a person can show is to die for his friends." (John 15:13)

This is just what God did for you and me. He came to earth in human form and allowed Himself to be crucified to take the punishment for the wrong things we have

done. In other words, God changed places with you and me. He made the first gesture of friendship by dying on that hill outside of Jerusalem.

Like any other friendship, a friendship with God is one that cannot simply be accepted; it must be returned. God has offered His friendship and we must say to Him in our hearts, "Yes, I want to be friends too."

The friendship with God does have some similarities to your friendship with other kids. Consider these:

the need to communicate

What kind of friendship would you have if you never spoke to your friend? A lousy one at best. God wants to hear from you. You can tell Him anything, no matter how silly or insignificant. He likes to hear about all the small details of your life as well as the big or heavy stuff.

Some people make the mistake of thinking that they only need to talk to God when they have problems or a bucket of sins to dump at His door for forgiveness. Nah! God loves to hear about the things that interest you. After all, how would you like to have a friend talk to you only when she has a problem she wants to be bailed out of? You would start to feel like a big fire escape, wouldn't you?

The act of talking to God is called *prayer*. And guess what? You can pray at any time. You don't even need to shut your eyes, fold your hands, or get down on your knees. You can talk silently to God—He can hear your thoughts—or you can bellow to Him out loud. You can pray as you walk to class; you can pray on the bus. Anywhere, any time, about anything.

And God wants to talk to you. Only rarely in history has God spoken in a voice that everyone could hear. He speaks through other people, circumstances, and His creation. Most often, He speaks through the Bible. It is the Word of God.

For some people, reading the Bible seems like a hassle. But think of it this way: suppose that a friend of yours writes you a note or shoots you an e-mail. What will you do when you receive it? Will you sit on it? Throw it away or delete it before reading it? Will you save it until Christmas? No way! You'll tear into that message and read it as soon as you can.

Well, the Best Friend you'll ever have has written you a note. It contains some very personal stuff about your life. If you take the time to read it, you'll grow to appreciate your friendship with God even more.

One word of caution: this note is a very long one; don't try to read it all at once. Read a little bit at a time. You'll be amazed at how God speaks to you.

the need for faithfulness

We damage our friendship with God when we ignore Him or put anything before Him. In a human relationship if you run out on your friends every time something a little more interesting comes along, your friendships will not last long. If you are too busy or involved with other activities to pay any attention to your friends, you'll find that they evaporate. God will not evaporate like that, but did you know that you can hurt His feelings? Check out Ephesians 4:30—"And do not make the Holy Spirit sad." Be very careful not to do anything that might harm your friendship with God.

the need to share your friend

A special friendship with God is something to be shared with others. God is big enough to give special attention to everyone who wants to be His friend. Tell other people by your words and actions about your relationship to your Creator!

one final, last word

This special friendship with God is one that will outlast any of the human friendships that you make. Even your very best

of friends will disappoint you from time to time. They won't come through when you really need them. But God will never ever fail you. Even though you may not always be able to understand what He is doing and why He is doing it, rest assured that He loves you and wants what's best for you—not only as you enter Middle School, but as you live the rest of your life!

plugging in

God did not design His children to be orphans. He made us to be part of his human family called the church. And probably like your family, the church is filled with all kinds of... um, "unique" people—weird uncles, odd tottering old people, snot-nosed kids, etc.

Sunday mornings are like big family meals—it's when everyone gets together to worship and learn about God.

Most churches also have a special group just for kids your age. They are called "youth groups" (although many youth groups give themselves special cool names). You really need to make being part of a youth group one of your top priorities each week. And believe me, many interests; homework, sports, hobbies, clubs etc. will try to compete with youth group for your time.

But your church youth group is far more important than those other important activities because your youth group is where you will get a chance to explore ideas about God. You'll learn His rules and values for living a worthwhile life, and you'll discover His love for you in a way that you can easily understand.

In your youth group there will be kids you would never normally hang out with. There will be some who say that he or she is a Christian, but who act in a completely different way. There will be kids who, like you, are trying to walk with God and learn more about Him, but don't always get it right.

In your youth group you will talk about stuff that really matters and get lots of great advice. You'll probably have a cool, older guide—your youth leader—who will help you and will be a trusted adult who understands, often better than your folks, what you are thinking and going through.